The 2019 San Francisco 49ers Complete Offensive Manual

Bobby Peters

DEDICATION

To Michelle and Mason.
To all those who have fostered a love of football in me.

TABLE OF CONTENTS

Introduction

Kyle Shanahan has been considered the top play designer / play caller in the NFL for a few years now. I have spent the last few years breaking down his tape in an effort to see how he destroyed the league in 2016 with Matt Ryan, and how he got the most out of the last two seasons with the 49ers. I thoroughly enjoyed the process of writing this book, and glad I finally had the chance to do so.

A "Bang Dig" is the term used in this book to describe the quick in cut (around 10-12 yards). This route is a staple in the Kyle Shanahan branch of the West Coast Offense. It is used in the play action game, as well as in the dropback pass game. This can be a 1 man route or a 2 man route (#2 runs a hitch, and often drifts out if covered to open up the dig window).

"Spot – Dig" is the general term I use for a 3 man dig combination. This concept is similar to the 2 man "Bang Dig", but uses an extra underneath route to hold both the flat defender and hook defender. Out of a 2x2 set, the flat will typically come from the back check-releasing. This action looks like the traditional Spot concept, hence the name.

All diagrams were created with JustPlay Sports Solutions. Their playbook software is an easy tool to use and has any feature you would want. I highly recommend using their product!

The concepts are based off of film study, and may be installed/taught differently by the 49ers. I pieced together each play based on my past experiences and what I saw on film.

While it does not have its own section, QB Sneaks were a huge part of the 49ers short yardage package. In $3^{rd}/4^{th}$ downs, the 49ers went 10 for 10 on converting QB Sneaks.

The fronts/coverages also have some room for interpretation. These have also been assigned based on film study without knowledge of each individual call. There may be some discrepancies here. Here is a quick summary of what each front term means:

- Over: Traditional definition. Bubble over strong guard. Nose in a weak 1/2i technique. Sam/Will can be walked up as well vs heavier personnel sets (typically)
- Under: Traditional definition. Bubble over weak guard. Nose in a strong 1/2i technique. Sam is typically walked up vs 21/22 personnel sets.
- Bear: Traditional definition. 3-0-3 with wide ends. No bubble.
- Wide: This front is typically used on pass downs. The ends are in 5's, and the nose/tackles are in 3's.
- Odd: Traditional Okie front. 4-0-4. 4i's are included here as well.
- Mug: All gaps are covered (with walked up linebackers). Typically on passing downs.

Here are the coverage definitions used. Within each general coverage, there are many variations.

- Cover 0: Man with no help. Typically paired with all out blitzes. In the low red zone, cover 0 is typically accompanied with a robber help inside.
- Cover 1: Man with a free safety help over the top. Some bracket coverages are included here as well.
- Cover 2: Traditional Cover 2 and Tampa 2
- Cover 3: Spot Drop Cover 3 and Zone Match Cover 3
- Cover 4: Quarters
- Cover 5: Man under two deep. This category also includes bracket coverage.

There are a few bunch checks that are referenced in this book. Here is a quick summary of each:

- Lock and Level: True man coverage
- Point/Traffic: man to man on the point man, other defenders play 1st inside and 1st outside.
- Box: Gets the defense 4 over 3. More of a true zone response. A good diagram of this can be seen at the end of the Double Digs section.

With the difference between outside zone and mid zone being hard to differentiate at times, these plays have been grouped together as "Outside Zone". I define mid zone as the frontside blocks looking more like inside zone, and the backside blockers reaching which looks more like true outside zone. The mid zone plays are typically run to the weak side.

When comparing inside zone to outside/mid zone, it is important to understand that a few clips may have accidentally been crossed over into the other category. With the similarities between plays and the sheer volume of cutups of this concept, a mistake or two may have occurred.

The 49ers often combined each individual quick game (3-step) concept with a wide variety of other quick game concepts. These are often referred to as "dual" reads. A dual read has the quarterback pick a side pre-snap, or immediately post snap after late safety rotation. These plays are not pure progression reads that cross the middle of the field.

With so much motion used throughout the season, it was not practical to include it within each diagram. Certain plays show the motion when it is critical to the concept. The next section shows the most common motions and why the 49ers used them.

If there are a couple concepts that you would like a cutup of, do not hesitate to contact me for them. My DM's are open on twitter, and my email is bpeters1212@gmail.com

General Notes

- The label "TO" in the charts stands for Turnover.
- The blank down and distance plays are two point conversion attempts.

- PA = Play Action
- "Fin" Route = 5 yard in (the route from #1 in Levels)

Common Motions

H Out Wide to Empty

- This motion is most commonly used with 10/11 personnel sets. In years past, Shanahan has used it with 12 personnel 2 TE surfaces as well.
- Forces a late empty check. Potential for a coverage miscommunication.
- Defense might have to check out of a certain blitz.

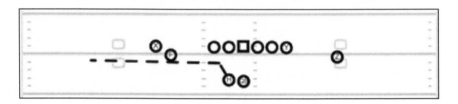

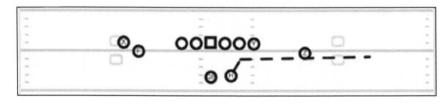

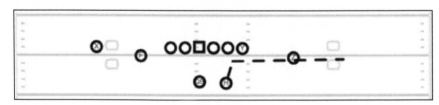

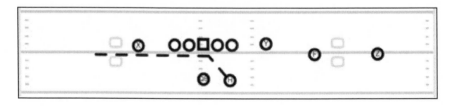

Tight End Motion to Opposite Side

- This motion is ideal for manipulating the defensive front to get a preferable look in the run game. In week 11, this motion was often used to get the 3 technique to the tight end side. Typically the Cardinals would call their under front in this matchup.
- This motion is also used for teams that like to spin down a safety pre-snap to the tight end. The motion gets the offense a better look to run to the tight end.
- This motion is used in the second diagram to either keep a defense from making a trips check, or to force late communication for the check.

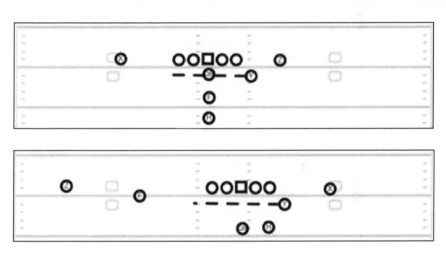

Running Back "Bounce"

- Defenses will sometimes set their front to the location of the running back. Bouncing him just before the snap does not let the interior of the defensive line reset. If they attempt to reset, the ball could potentially be snapped before they are ready.

- When the 49ers free release the running back, the bouncing can sometimes change coverage responsibilities very quickly before the ball is snapped.

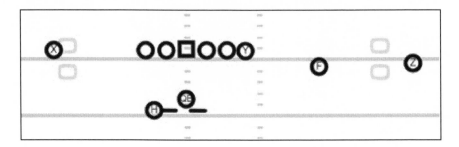

Running Back "Home"/"Reload"

- This motion gets the defense into a pre-snap empty check, and forces them to communicate back out of it.
- Reloading the running back can get the defense out of a blitz call with the initial empty check. Even after the reload, the call may still be off.
- If a blitz is called as the empty check, the blitz might not be as effective when the back reloads. If the defense leaves the empty check blitz on, they may get burned.

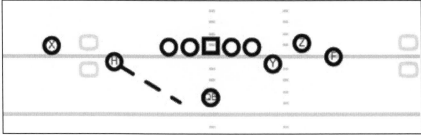

Fullback Shuffle Motion

- This motion can give the fullback a better angle at his kickout block on power or leading to the edge for outside zone schemes.
- The motion can also be used as an element of misdirection. Shuffle one way, and run a counter or other scheme back the other way.
  - Shuffle to a strong alignment, run counter the other way.
  - Shuffle to a strong alignment, run zone slice to the side of the shuffle.
  - Shuffle back to a straight I, Run zone lead where the shuffle came from.
- When commonly used to create advantages in the run game, the shuffle motion can spice up the play action game as well.
- This motion can create free releases for the full back or running back in the pass game as well. The motion can get the back outside the tackle faster for their choice routes from an under center formation.

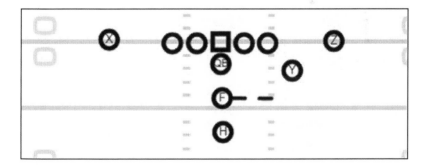

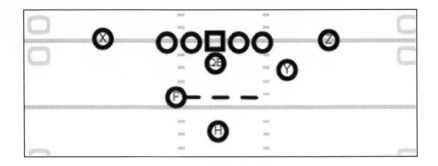

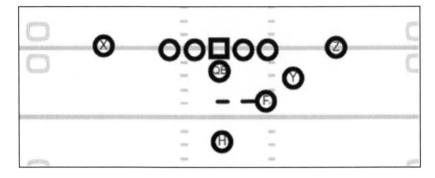

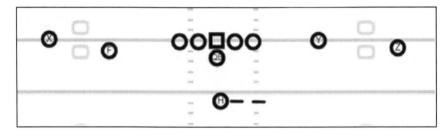

Run Game Overview

Kyle Shanahan has the most expansive run game in the NFL. The 49ers executed many schemes at a high level during the season, a testament to the level of detail in the coaching.

In general, the outside zone blocking rules can be understood based on the position of the defender in the play side gap next to an offensive lineman. If there is somebody in your play side gap, that's your guy. If he is closer to you than the offensive lineman towards your gap, that is typically a 1 on 1 block. If he is closer to your play side teammate, your teammate will combo with you until you can over take. This is illustrated in the "Outside Zone – Strong – Lead" section with the play drawn up against an Over front. The play side guard will block the 3 technique 1 on 1. The back side guard and center combo the back side 1 technique.

In odd fronts (think 4-0-4) where the center and both tackles have guys head up from them, the man on and behind will combo together. This is drawn up in the "Outside Zone – Strong – Lead" section.

There are a few wrinkles to the zone running system. When the 49ers run it to the weak side of the formation (without a tight end), the play side tackle will essentially use inside zone footwork and not reach his guy. This way of running zone is often referred to as "mid zone". For the purpose of this book, all of these concepts are titled with outside zone in their title.

On the front side of most run plays, the wide receiver, if aligned in a condensed split, will block the force player. This is an important element in the 49ers run game. The image below shows what this looks like for a zone run.

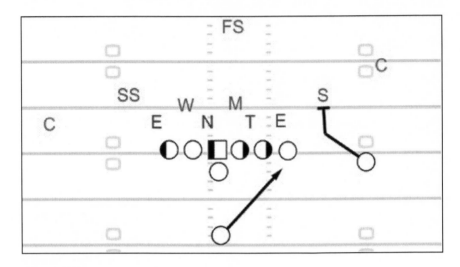

The 49ers use different tempos and cadences constantly. Both of these have a strong impact on the running game. For example, the 49ers will break the huddle and get to the line quickly and snap the ball on first sound to run outside zone. The tempo and cadence gives the offensive line a better chance to get their reach block handled. A good example of this can be found in the Super Bowl in the "Outside Zone Strong Slice" section. The backside guard is able to reach a 1 technique without help because he gets a head start with the quick snap count. .

In interviews, Shanahan has talked about his audibles/kills. In his system, they are referred to as "cans". Two plays will be called in the huddle, if the first one doesn't work on paper, they will "can" to the 2nd play. They will use this method on about half of their plays. They have certain plays they will not check out of. If you watch the broadcast version of the game, you can hear Garoppolo most of the time when he calls these out.

They will also have the 2nd play be a shot play against a certain coverage. This is the case for the long double move to Kittle in week 12. Garoppolo sees quarters, and calls out "can-can, can-can" at the line of scrimmage.

In the next few pages, you will find a run game overview for each game. Their top eight runs have been included. All variations of each run are included.

Week 1 vs TB				Week 2 vs CIN			
Outside Zone		Inside Zone		Outside Zone		Inside Zone	
Called	Average	Called	Average	Called	Average	Called	Average
10	2.1	9	2.9	8	7.1	10	7.8
Power		Counter		Power		Counter	
Called	Average	Called	Average	Called	Average	Called	Average
0	0.0	2	11.5	2	3.5	5	5.2
Crack Toss		Duo		Crack Toss		Duo	
Called	Average	Called	Average	Called	Average	Called	Average
3	2.3	4	4.3	1	11.0	0	0.0
Trap		Pin/Pull		Trap		Pin/Pull	
Called	Average	Called	Average	Called	Average	Called	Average
0	0.0	0	0.0	0	0.0	0	0.0

Week 3 vs PIT				Week 5 vs CLE			
Outside Zone		Inside Zone		Outside Zone		Inside Zone	
Called	Average	Called	Average	Called	Average	Called	Average
9	5.6	11	3.3	13	4.9	5	2.0
Power		Counter		Power		Counter	
Called	Average	Called	Average	Called	Average	Called	Average
3	8.3	7	6.7	2	5.0	6	2.0
Crack Toss		Duo		Crack Toss		Duo	
Called	Average	Called	Average	Called	Average	Called	Average
1	-18.0	2	0.0	2	9.0	0	0.0
Trap		Pin/Pull		Trap		Pin/Pull	
Called	Average	Called	Average	Called	Average	Called	Average
0	0.0	2	7.5	2	5.5	1	19.0

Week 6 vs LAR				Week 7 vs WAS			
Outside Zone		Inside Zone		Outside Zone		Inside Zone	
Called	Average	Called	Average	Called	Average	Called	Average
13	2.2	5	2.4	15	4.6	5	2.8
Power		Counter		Power		Counter	
Called	Average	Called	Average	Called	Average	Called	Average
5	3.6	4	2.8	1	2.0	3	2.7
Crack Toss		Duo		Crack Toss		Duo	
Called	Average	Called	Average	Called	Average	Called	Average
3	1.7	8	3.9	0	0.0	5	3.8
Trap		Pin/Pull		Trap		Pin/Pull	
Called	Average	Called	Average	Called	Average	Called	Average
0	0.0	0	0.0	1	2.0	2	-0.5

Week 8 vs CAR				Week 9 vs ARI			
Outside Zone		Inside Zone		Outside Zone		Inside Zone	
Called	Average	Called	Average	Called	Average	Called	Average
19	6.0	5	2.6	15	3.8	2	-2.0
Power		Counter		Power		Counter	
Called	Average	Called	Average	Called	Average	Called	Average
2	-0.5	3	9.3	4	4.3	1	1.0
Crack Toss		Duo		Crack Toss		Duo	
Called	Average	Called	Average	Called	Average	Called	Average
2	9.0	1	3.0	4	5.5	0	0.0
Trap		Pin/Pull		Trap		Pin/Pull	
Called	Average	Called	Average	Called	Average	Called	Average
4	18.0	0	0.0	3	2.0	0	0.0

Week 10 vs SEA				Week 11 vs ARI			
Outside Zone		Inside Zone		Outside Zone		Inside Zone	
Called	Average	Called	Average	Called	Average	Called	Average
13	6.0	3	1.7	5	1.0	3	2.0
Power		Counter		Power		Counter	
Called	Average	Called	Average	Called	Average	Called	Average
1	2.0	7	3.1	5	2.0	0	0.0
Crack Toss		Duo		Crack Toss		Duo	
Called	Average	Called	Average	Called	Average	Called	Average
0	0.0	0	0.0	0	0.0	1	4.0
Trap		Pin/Pull		Trap		Pin/Pull	
Called	Average	Called	Average	Called	Average	Called	Average
0	0.0	4	0.3	1	-1.0	0	0.0

Week 12 vs GB				Week 13 vs BAL			
Outside Zone		Inside Zone		Outside Zone		Inside Zone	
Called	Average	Called	Average	Called	Average	Called	Average
4	1.5	5	7.2	17	7.4	1	3.0
Power		Counter		Power		Counter	
Called	Average	Called	Average	Called	Average	Called	Average
1	5.0	1	2.0	2	1.5	0	0.0
Crack Toss		Duo		Crack Toss		Duo	
Called	Average	Called	Average	Called	Average	Called	Average
0	0.0	3	3.3	1	6.0	0	0.0
Trap		Pin/Pull		Trap		Pin/Pull	
Called	Average	Called	Average	Called	Average	Called	Average
3	14.7	1	6.0	0	0.0	0	0.0

Week 14 vs NO				Week 15 vs ATL			
Outside Zone		Inside Zone		Outside Zone		Inside Zone	
Called	Average	Called	Average	Called	Average	Called	Average
8	5.0	5	6.8	8	8.9	7	4.6
Power		Counter		Power		Counter	
Called	Average	Called	Average	Called	Average	Called	Average
1	3.0	2	2.5	0	0.0	0	0.0
Crack Toss		Duo		Crack Toss		Duo	
Called	Average	Called	Average	Called	Average	Called	Average
1	6.0	1	0.0	3	1.3	2	5.5
Trap		Pin/Pull		Trap		Pin/Pull	
Called	Average	Called	Average	Called	Average	Called	Average
3	5.7	0	0.0	3	3.3	1	16.0

Week 16 vs LAR				Week 17 vs SEA			
Outside Zone		Inside Zone		Outside Zone		Inside Zone	
Called	Average	Called	Average	Called	Average	Called	Average
8	5.0	2	8.5	6	8.3	6	3.0
Power		Counter		Power		Counter	
Called	Average	Called	Average	Called	Average	Called	Average
1	9.0	2	4.0	2	7.0	0	0.0
Crack Toss		Duo		Crack Toss		Duo	
Called	Average	Called	Average	Called	Average	Called	Average
0	0.0	2	1.0	0	0.0	0	0.0
Trap		Pin/Pull		Trap		Pin/Pull	
Called	Average	Called	Average	Called	Average	Called	Average
3	6.3	0	0.0	2	4.0	3	1.7

DIV vs MIN				NFCCG vs GB			
Outside Zone		Inside Zone		Outside Zone		Inside Zone	
Called	Average	Called	Average	Called	Average	Called	Average
25	4.4	4	3.0	16	8.7	4	3.8
Power		Counter		Power		Counter	
Called	Average	Called	Average	Called	Average	Called	Average
2	6.5	5	4.6	5	0.8	4	3.8
Crack Toss		Duo		Crack Toss		Duo	
Called	Average	Called	Average	Called	Average	Called	Average
0	0.0	2	1.0	1	5.0	1	0.0
Trap		Pin/Pull		Trap		Pin/Pull	
Called	Average	Called	Average	Called	Average	Called	Average
4	5.0	0	0.0	5	11.2	1	9.0

SB vs KC			
Outside Zone		Inside Zone	
Called	Average	Called	Average
11	7.8	2	1.5
Power		Counter	
Called	Average	Called	Average
4	2.5	2	2.0
Crack Toss		Duo	
Called	Average	Called	Average
2	6.5	0	0.0
Trap		Pin/Pull	
Called	Average	Called	Average
0	0.0	0	0.0

Outside Zone – Strong – Lead

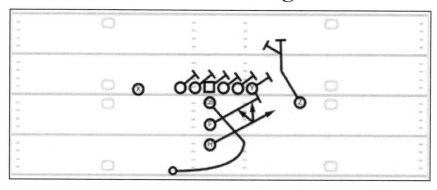

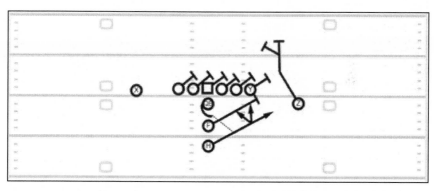

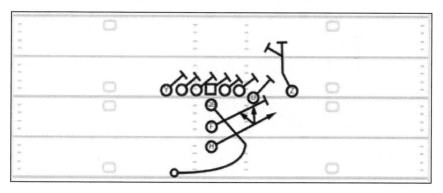

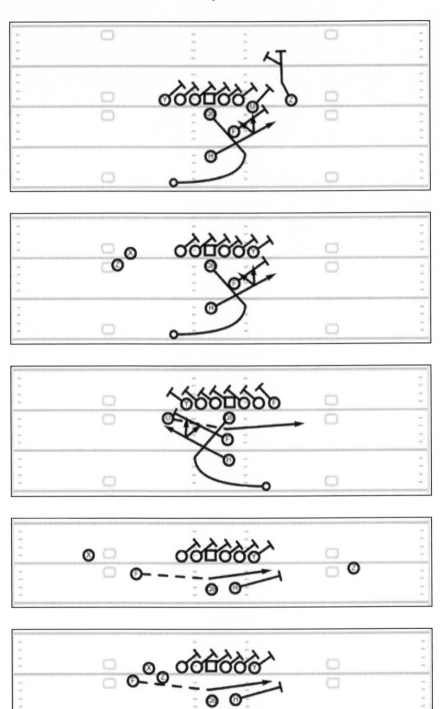

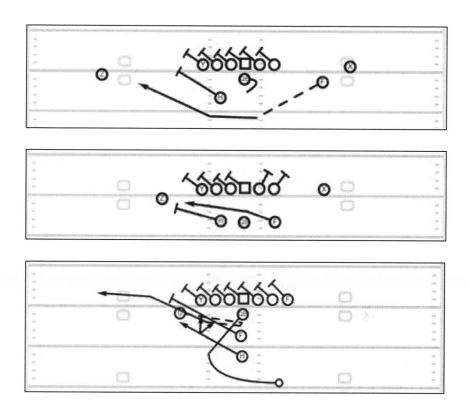

Week	Quarter	Time	Down	ToGo	Location	Yards
Week 1 vs TB	2	11:14	2	10	SFO 8	-2
Week 1 vs TB	2	9:12	2	9	SFO 21	1
Week 1 vs TB	2	2:19	2	5	TAM 24	4
Week 1 vs TB	3	4:34	1	10	SFO 48	8
Week 2 vs CIN	2	6:22	1	10	CIN 37	1
Week 2 vs CIN	3	9:12	1	10	SFO 31	7
Week 2 vs CIN	3	8:45	2	3	SFO 38	18
Week 2 vs CIN	3	8:04	1	10	CIN 44	1
Week 2 vs CIN	3	2:21	1	10	CIN 46	6
Week 3 vs PIT	**2**	**15:00**	**2**	**7**	**PIT 25**	**10**
Week 3 vs PIT	**3**	**12:41**	**2**	**5**	**PIT 33**	**6**
Week 3 vs PIT	4	14:01	1	10	SFO 25	3
Week 3 vs PIT	4	12:47	2	26	SFO 9	3
Week 3 vs PIT	4	9:47	1	10	PIT 43	5
Week 5 vs CLE	3	14:32	2	2	SFO 18	-4
Week 5 vs CLE	3	3:10	2	7	CLE 39	19
Week 5 vs CLE	4	2:54	2	7	SFO 23	2
Week 6 vs LA	2	8:44	1	10	SFO 11	-2
Week 6 vs LA	3	9:21	1	10	RAM 39	3
Week 7 vs WAS	4	6:42	1	10	SFO 33	3
Week 7 vs WAS	4	5:59	2	7	SFO 36	3
Week 8 vs CAR	1	11:10	1	10	CAR 19	2
Week 9 vs ARI	2	4:14	2	5	SFO 25	31
Week 9 vs ARI	2	1:48	1	5	CRD 5	2
Week 9 vs ARI	3	3:27	1	10	SFO 39	3
Week 9 vs ARI	4	2:21	1	10	CRD 49	-2
Week 10 vs SEA	1	5:03	1	10	SEA 26	2
Week 10 vs SEA	**2**	**8:44**	**1**	**10**	**SFO 37**	**7**
Week 10 vs SEA	3	7:07	1	10	SFO 30	3
Week 10 vs SEA	3	0:59	2	2	SFO 33	1
Week 10 vs SEA	4	9:03	1	10	SEA 41	8
Week 10 vs SEA	OT	5:34	1	10	SEA 49	4

Week	Quarter	Time	Down	ToGo	Location	Yards
Week 11 vs ARI	1	10:05	2	6	SFO 29	1
Week 11 vs ARI	1	0:34	2	11	SFO 14	2
Week 11 vs ARI	2	2:44	1	10	CRD 46	2
Week 12 vs GB	4	11:29	1	10	SFO 31	-2
Week 13 vs BAL	**1**	**13:01**	**1**	**10**	**RAV 41**	**8**
Week 13 vs BAL	3	0:50	2	7	SFO 4	3
Week 14 vs NO	4	13:50	1	10	NOR 47	-1
Week 15 vs ATL	**1**	**7:06**	**1**	**10**	**SFO 28**	**8**
Week 16 vs LAR	2	14:55	1	10	SFO 25	9
Week 16 vs LAR	2	6:20	2	10	SFO 38	0
Week 16 vs LAR	**2**	**5:06**	**1**	**10**	**SFO 50**	**5**
Week 16 vs LAR	3	13:53	1	10	SFO 42	6
Week 17 vs SEA	**1**	**9:57**	**1**	**10**	**SEA 45**	**17**
Week 17 vs SEA	**1**	**3:00**	**1**	**10**	**SFO 16**	**3**
Week 17 vs SEA	**3**	**15:00**	**1**	**10**	**SFO 25**	**-1**
Week 17 vs SEA	3	3:28	2	2	SEA 2	2
DIV vs MIN	1	5:23	1	10	SFO 25	6
DIV vs MIN	2	10:33	2	4	MIN 35	5
DIV vs MIN	2	9:51	1	10	MIN 30	7
DIV vs MIN	**2**	**7:13**	**2**	**1**	**MIN 1**	**1**
DIV vs MIN	3	12:18	1	10	MIN 25	6
DIV vs MIN	**4**	**2:29**	**1**	**10**	**SFO 40**	**6**
DIV vs MIN	**4**	**2:00**	**2**	**4**	**SFO 46**	**2**
NFCCG vs GB	**1**	**8:53**	**1**	**10**	**SFO 27**	**5**
NFCCG vs GB	1	2:16	1	10	SFO 49	4
NFCCG vs GB	**2**	**12:32**	**1**	**10**	**GNB 37**	**13**
NFCCG vs GB	2	5:35	1	10	SFO 31	34
NFCCG vs GB	2	4:57	1	10	GNB 35	7
NFCCG vs GB	3	5:21	1	10	GNB 22	0
NFCCG vs GB	4	7:24	1	10	SFO 46	5
NFCCG vs GB	4	6:40	2	5	GNB 49	2
SB vs KC	1	13:55	1	10	SFO 18	-1
SB vs KC	2	8:09	1	10	SFO 30	16
SB vs KC	3	11:14	2	5	KAN 27	0

Average Yards per Play	5.0

1st Down		3rd/4th Down (includes RZ)	
Called	Average	Called	Success Rate
47	5.1	0	0%
2nd Down 6-1		**2nd Down 7+**	
Called	Average	Called	Average
15	5.3	10	4.1
Red Zone 10-0		**Red Zone 10-20**	
Called	Touchdown %	Called	Touchdown %
3	67%	1	0%

Bear		Over	
Called	Average	Called	Average
15	6.8	24	5.4
Under		**Mug**	
Called	Average	Called	Average
24	4.0	1	1.0
Wide		**Odd**	
Called	Average	Called	Average
1	0.0	7	4.7

Running outside zone to the strong side, with the addition of a lead blocker, removes the need for the offense to check out of this play.

The 49ers will toss the ball on this play as well.

The diagram below shows the play against an over front. The key front side block is the play side guard 1 on 1 with the 3 technique. The combination block from the tight end and the play side tackle is critical as well, as the play has good potential to hit outside against this front.

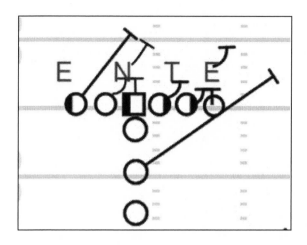

The diagram below shows the concept against an odd front. Hard slanting 4's and 4i's can make the frontside, and especially the backside, blocks tricky. Against two-gapping teams, the combo blocks become easier with more passive fronts. The fullback has a little navigating to do on this one. If the tight end cannot reach the Sam, the fullback will have to cut inside his block.

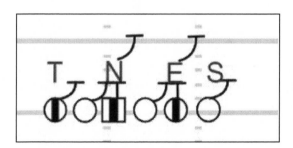

Against more true bear looks, the frontside blocks look like they would against an over front. The play side guard will take the 3 technique by himself, and the tight end and tackle will combo the edge. The center is left by himself on the nose so that the back side guard can help the tackle with sealing the backside 3 technique.

The plays bolded are variations where the fullback blocks
the first guy outside of the tight end, and the tight end
climbs. These plays are designed to get the ball to the
sideline even when the defense plays with a sam on the ball.
With this version called, the toss action is used. The image
below shows the play.

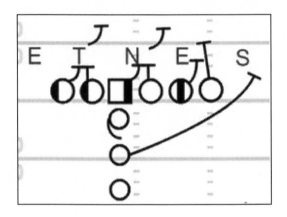

With the fullback blocking the first man outside the tight
end, the play will look like power to the outside linebacker.
In week 16 2Q 5:06, the linebacker tires to spill the
fullback, which allowed the RB to get outside.

Within this section, there are a number of ways Shanahan
runs this version of outside zone. With the sam linebacker
on the ball, there is a variation where the fullback will give
inside help for the tight end, and even take the sam if he
jumps inside the tight end.

In the low red zone, the 49ers used a fake jet motion away
from the run and a return flat motion to the same side as
the run in week 17 and in the divisional round for
touchdowns. The motion from week 17 pulled an extra

defender to the flat. These versions can be seen in the 6th and 11th diagrams.

The jet sweep variations have bene included in this section as well. The use of 11 personnel is a great way to get the edge with this play. Many teams will play a softer edge and not have the sam on the against these looks. The tight end and tackle will combo the defensive end, and the lead blocker will pick up the force player.

Why it Worked: In week 2 3Q 8:45 the play side 3 tech gets reached and the play hits B gap for a big gain.

The 8 yard gain in week 1 shows a nice combo with the play side tackle and tight end. The play side guard reaches the 3 technique with ease (sensing a theme with the 3 techniques?).

The nineteen yarder in week 5 shows another nice combo with the frontside tackle and tight end.

The 49ers get Samuel on the jet sweep version or a nice gain in the Super Bowl.

Why it Didn't Work: As a front side 3 technique, Aaron Donald makes a signature play by ripping inside the guard and making the play in the backfield in week 6.

In week 5, the running back tried taking the ball outside vs a hard edge 9 technique.

Outside Zone Weak – Lead

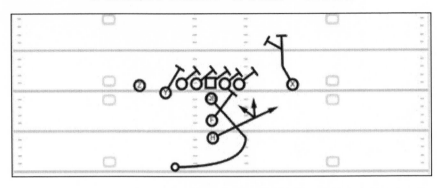

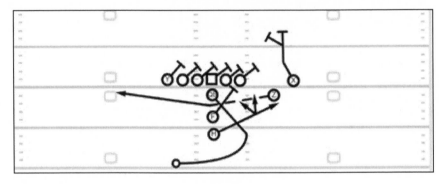

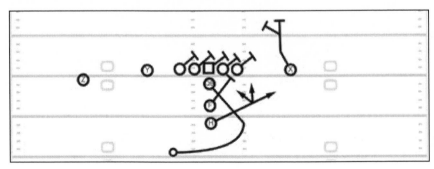

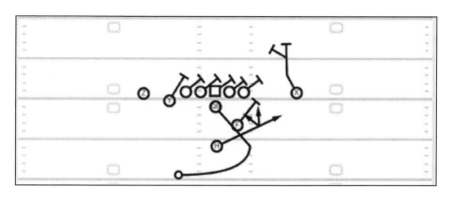

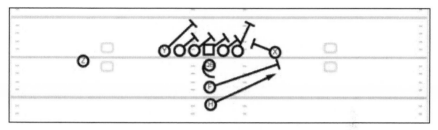

Average Yards per Play	4.4

1st Down		3rd/4th Down (includes RZ)	
Called	Average	Called	Success Rate
10	3.6	0	0%
2nd Down 6-1		**2nd Down 7+**	
Called	Average	Called	Average
0	0.0	6	5.8
Red Zone 10-0		**Red Zone 10-20**	
Called	Touchdown %	Called	Touchdown %
0	0%	2	0%

Bear		Over	
Called	Average	Called	Average
1	6.0	4	2.0
Under		**Mug**	
Called	Average	Called	Average
9	5.7	0	0.0
Wide		**Odd**	
Called	Average	Called	Average
0	0.0	2	3.0

Week	Quarter	Time	Down	ToGo	Location	Yards
Week 2 vs CIN	3	14:24	1	10	CIN 36	6
Week 3 vs PIT	1	11:40	1	10	SFO 25	4
Week 6 vs LA	3	8:48	2	7	RAM 36	1
Week 7 vs WAS	3	10:05	1	10	SFO 23	2
Week 8 vs CAR	1	15:00	1	10	SFO 25	1
Week 9 vs ARI	2	11:48	1	10	SFO 44	11
Week 9 vs ARI	2	4:58	1	10	SFO 20	5
Week 9 vs ARI	2	2:13	1	10	CRD 14	3
Week 9 vs ARI	3	14:50	2	10	SFO 28	4
Week 9 vs ARI	4	7:47	1	10	SFO 33	-2
Week 10 vs SEA	1	2:42	2	12	SEA 14	4
Week 10 vs SEA	1	0:31	1	10	SFO 26	0
Week 12 vs GB	1	0:39	2	8	SFO 39	2
Week 14 vs NO	1	4:00	2	14	SFO 21	2
DIV vs MIN	3	3:26	1	10	SFO 17	6
NFCCG vs GB	3	4:56	2	10	GNB 22	22

The Outside Zone – Weak – Lead is a tendency breaker for the Outside Zone – Strong – Lead.

This version will use the "Mid Zone" style of front side blocking. The front side tackle will base block the 5 technique, and the back will try and hit the play inside of him. The running back's big read here is the play side 3 technique.

This play was most commonly called and gamed planned for under fronts. Against an under front, the key combo is the center and backside guard on the 1 technique. The play is shown below.

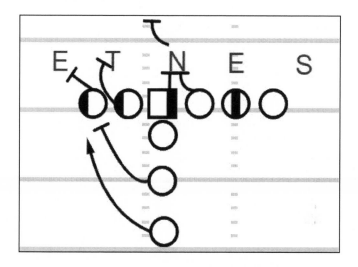

This version was a big part of the week 9 game plan with the Cardinals heavy usage of the under front.

The 11 yard gain in week 9 is shown in the 5th diagram. This play has the X receiver crack the end man on the line of scrimmage, the front side tackle climb, and the fullback clean up the man to man corner. This version is a nice changeup to get the ball on the edge to the weak side. This variation was also used in week 12. The play is drawn below.

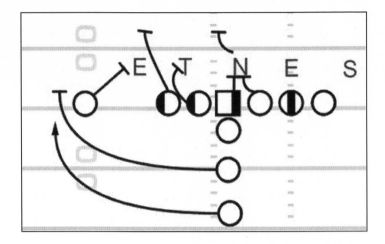

In this version, the play side guard MUST reach the 3 technique.

Why it Worked: A strong 1 on 1 block with the play side 3 technique is the key with this play. This was the case for the big week 2 run against a bear front (called back for holding).

Why it Didn't Work: Za Darius Smith sniffs out the crack block and spins out of it to occupy the FB and X receiver in the week 12 clip, and forced the fullback to take the edge player. The backside defensive end beats the tight end to take away the cutback in week 9 4Q 7:47.

Outside Zone Strong – 11 & 12 Personnel

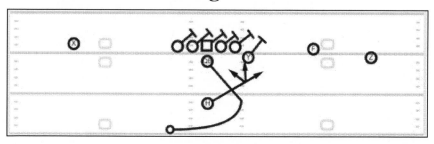

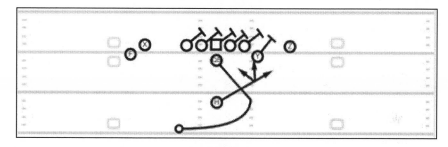

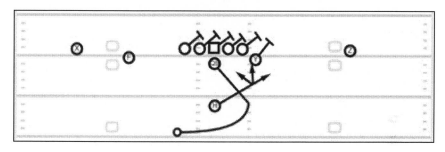

Average Yards per Play	5.1

1st Down		3rd/4th Down (includes RZ)	
Called	Average	Called	Success Rate
16	5.1	2	50%
2nd Down 6-1		**2nd Down 7+**	
Called	Average	Called	Average
6	4.0	4	7.0
Red Zone 10-0		**Red Zone 10-20**	
Called	Touchdown %	Called	Touchdown %
0	0%	4	25%

Bear		Over	
Called	Average	Called	Average
6	8.7	14	4.8
Under		**Mug**	
Called	Average	Called	Average
6	3.2	0	0.0
Wide		**Odd**	
Called	Average	Called	Average
0	0.0	2	3.0

Week	Quarter	Time	Down	ToGo	Location	Yards
Week 5 vs CLE	3	2:54	1	10	CLE 20	2
Week 5 vs CLE	3	1:02	1	10	SFO 10	5
Week 5 vs CLE	4	2:07	3	5	SFO 25	8
Week 6 vs LA	1	14:22	2	9	SFO 18	4
Week 6 vs LA	4	10:20	1	10	RAM 45	6
Week 6 vs LA	4	4:31	1	10	SFO 42	2
Week 7 vs WAS	4	3:31	1	10	WAS 30	6
Week 7 vs WAS	4	3:26	2	4	WAS 24	8
Week 7 vs WAS	4	2:40	1	10	WAS 16	0
Week 8 vs CAR	4	12:03	1	10	SFO 47	3
Week 9 vs ARI	1	12:05	1	10	SFO 23	0
Week 9 vs ARI	1	7:08	1	10	SFO 33	-1
Week 10 vs SEA	1	14:19	2	9	SFO 26	-1
Week 10 vs SEA	1	12:33	2	5	SFO 46	0
Week 10 vs SEA	1	12:16	2	10	SEA 49	4
Week 10 vs SEA	3	4:20	1	10	SFO 40	0
Week 12 vs GB	4	9:27	1	10	SFO 44	4
Week 13 vs BAL	1	7:57	1	10	SFO 27	2
Week 13 vs BAL	2	1:58	1	10	SFO 25	19
Week 13 vs BAL	2	0:32	2	12	SFO 42	16
Week 13 vs BAL	3	10:58	1	10	SFO 42	9
Week 13 vs BAL	4	7:58	2	7	RAV 41	3
Week 13 vs BAL	4	7:15	3	4	RAV 38	3
Week 14 vs NO	3	0:17	2	5	SFO 50	4
Week 15 vs ATL	4	11:48	2	5	SFO 33	2
Week 16 vs LAR	2	2:26	1	10	RAM 16	16
Week 16 vs LAR	3	12:04	2	5	RAM 39	-1
Week 17 vs SEA	1	4:09	2	10	SFO 6	5
DIV vs MIN	3	13:04	2	5	MIN 32	7
DIV vs MIN	3	9:09	2	6	MIN 40	6
DIV vs MIN	3	8:27	1	10	MIN 34	6
DIV vs MIN	3	6:21	2	6	MIN 17	4
SB vs KC	4	6:06	1	10	SFO 20	5

This concept was primarily called against over fronts. In 11 personnel, this is the most common front you will see.

This play is designed to get outside the tight end. The tight end and tackle will combo the defensive end to get up to the strong linebacker. The image below shows the play against an over front.

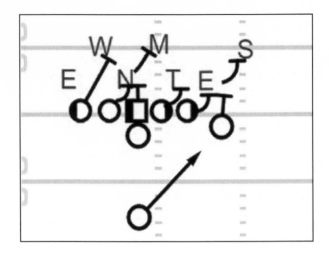

If the defense lines up with a 9 technique, the play will most likely have to cut back.

Why it Worked: The touchdown in week 16 was a timely play call, executed to perfection. The 49ers run strong against an over front with the OLB walked up weak. The front side 3 tech gets reached, and the center and back side guard combo the 1 tech beautifully. The play hits front side.

In week 13, the Ravens slant weak out of their bear front. This left them short on the front side, as nobody scrapped over the top. Week 7 shows a nice clip vs an odd front.

Why it Didn't Work: In week 5 3Q 2:54, the strong side of the D-line stunts inside, and the linebackers scrape hard over the top. In general, line movement that is sharply executed can give zone running teams trouble.

The play side 3 tech blows up the play in week 15.

Outside Zone Weak – 11 & 12 Personnel

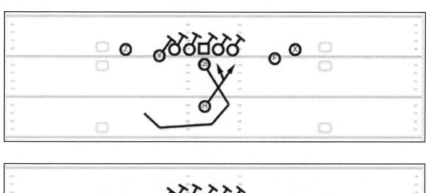

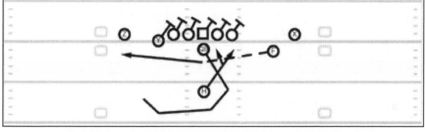

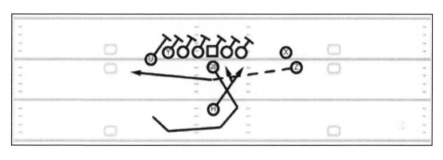

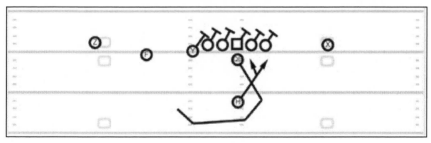

Average Yards per Play	3.9

1st Down		3rd/4th Down (includes RZ)	
Called	Average	Called	Success Rate
12	3.9	1	0%
2nd Down 6-1		2nd Down 7+	
Called	Average	Called	Average
2	1.0	7	4.4
Red Zone 10-0		Red Zone 10-20	
Called	Touchdown %	Called	Touchdown %
0	0%	1	100%

Bear		Over	
Called	Average	Called	Average
2	-1.0	13	4.8
Under		Mug	
Called	Average	Called	Average
5	2.8	0	0.0
Wide		Odd	
Called	Average	Called	Average
0	0.0	1	6.0

Week	Quarter	Time	Down	ToGo	Location	Yards
Week 1 vs TB	2	7:45	2	7	TAM 41	4
Week 1 vs TB	3	13:46	1	10	SFO 37	0
Week 1 vs TB	3	3:23	2	10	TAM 39	0
Week 1 vs TB	4	13:04	1	10	SFO 2	3
Week 3 vs PIT	2	9:35	1	10	PIT 26	4
Week 5 vs CLE	2	3:32	2	9	CLE 35	4
Week 5 vs CLE	3	0:17	2	5	SFO 15	-4
Week 7 vs WAS	4	1:15	3	11	WAS 17	6
Week 8 vs CAR	2	7:39	1	10	CAR 43	0
Week 8 vs CAR	3	10:04	1	10	SFO 37	6
Week 9 vs ARI	3	8:21	2	8	SFO 50	4
Week 9 vs ARI	4	4:47	1	10	SFO 26	-1
Week 10 vs SEA	1	14:19	2	9	SFO 26	-1
Week 11 vs ARI	2	4:46	1	5	SFO 25	0
Week 13 vs BAL	3	7:32	1	10	RAV 38	0
Week 14 vs NO	2	6:48	1	10	SFO 46	19
Week 14 vs NO	3	14:21	1	10	SFO 36	-1
Week 15 vs ATL	3	13:32	2	7	SFO 46	2
DIV vs MIN	3	9:09	2	6	MIN 40	6
DIV vs MIN	3	8:27	1	10	MIN 34	6
NFCCG vs GB	2	0:50	2	9	GNB 18	18
SB vs KC	2	7:19	1	10	SFO 46	11

This variation of outside zone falls into the mid zone category. The offense is not trying to reach a play side 5 tech, instead they are trying to hit a cutback lane.

Similar to the back side "lock" tag, this variation hinges upon the ability of the interior of the offensive line to get their reach blocks. Additionally, the running back has to have a strong feel for the cutback aspect of the play.

This play is designed to hit the front side B gap bubble against over fronts. Sean McVay and the Rams rode this as their base play to the Super Bowl in 2018. Taylor Kolste does a great job breaking this play down in his Rams book, and the many intricacies they used for it. For the 49ers, it was a smaller part of their offense.

There are a few clips where the defense slants away from the run. These can be seen in 2Q and 4Q week 1 and week 15.

Why it Worked: In week 14, the defensive end loses contain and the play bounces outside for a big gain. The receiver does a nice job of blocking the hard cover 2 corner.

Why it Didn't Work: In week 11, both the 1 tech and 5 tech slip under their blocks to get the running back cutting back

In week 5, the center struggled reaching the play side 1 tech.

In week 9, the running back misses a cutback opportunity, and the play gets strung out to the sideline.

Outside Zone Slice – 11 Personnel

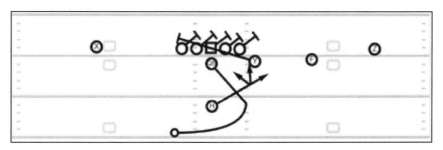

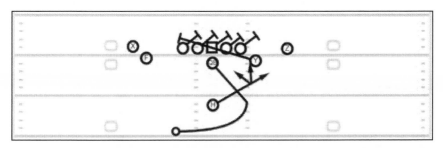

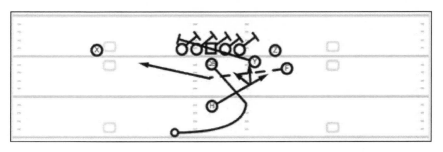

Bear		Over	
Called	Average	Called	Average
2	1.5	7	7.1
Under		Mug	
Called	Average	Called	Average
7	2.4	0	0.0
Wide		Odd	
Called	Average	Called	Average
2	9.0	2	6.0

Average Yards per Play	4.8

1st Down		3rd/4th Down (includes RZ)	
Called	Average	Called	Success Rate
11	8.1	3	0%
2nd Down 6-1		**2nd Down 7+**	
Called	Average	Called	Average
1	0.0	6	0.3
Red Zone 10-0		**Red Zone 10-20**	
Called	Touchdown %	Called	Touchdown %
2	0%	0	0%

Week	Quarter	Time	Down	ToGo	Location	Yards
Week 1 vs TB	2	7:02	3	3	TAM 37	1
Week 5 vs CLE	4	7:02	1	15	CLE 34	14
Week 5 vs CLE	4	5:52	2	11	CLE 30	4
Week 6 vs LA	2	7:20	3	18	SFO 3	7
Week 6 vs LA	4	4:19	3	8	SFO 44	2
Week 7 vs WAS	1	1:58	1	10	SFO 46	1
Week 7 vs WAS	2	1:23	1	10	SFO 34	11
Week 7 vs WAS	4	10:49	1	7	WAS 7	3
Week 7 vs WAS	4	4:27	1	10	WAS 45	9
Week 8 vs CAR	2	0:11	2	8	SFO 27	-1
Week 8 vs CAR	4	11:17	2	7	SFO 50	-2
Week 8 vs CAR	4	6:24	1	10	CAR 41	41
Week 8 vs CAR	4	4:08	1	10	CAR 41	2
Week 9 vs ARI	2	9:46	2	6	CRD 7	0
Week 10 vs SEA	4	14:56	2	10	SFO 36	-1
Week 12 vs GB	1	1:17	1	10	SFO 37	2
Week 13 vs BAL	1	7:18	2	8	SFO 29	2
Week 13 vs BAL	2	11:23	1	10	SFO 45	0
Week 14 vs NO	4	4:14	1	10	NOR 34	4
Week 15 vs ATL	1	12:00	1	10	SFO 20	2
DIV vs MIN	1	2:51	2	10	SFO 48	0

This 11 personnel variation is a good way to attack over/under fronts. This variation was called five times in the 49ers Week 8 win vs the Carolina Panthers. The Panthers line up in an Over front a vast majority of the time, with some under fronts mixed in. The diagram below shows the concept against an Over front.

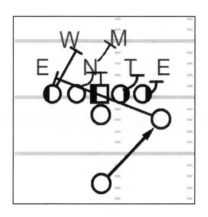

The goal of the play is to hit the cutback just behind the backside tackle's block. If the weak linebacker doesn't "fall back" and stay outside the backside tackle, the cutback lane is huge. The 3rd & 18 in week 6 is a good example of this, even though the 49ers did not convert.

NFL defenses are pretty accustomed to defending this action, so the huge cutback is typically not the case.

The 49ers had some big plays hitting the front side of the play in 2019. The 41 yard touchdown in week 8 vs Carolina is a great example. This play is the 3rd diagram shown, with fake jet motion. The fake jet motion forces the defense to "fall back" twice on the same play. Out of this formation, the nickel will have to fit the front side A gap (in an Over front). This was the case on this particular play. The Nickel got lost, leaving a huge lane for the running back.

Why it Worked: The big gainer from week 8 is explained above. In week 5, the front side B gap linebacker runs himself out of the play and the center gets a nice reach on the play side 1 tech. In week 7, Washington loops their play side end around to the A gap and the 49ers bounce this one outside.

Why it Didn't Work: The corner makes a nice tackle on the 3rd down in week 1. The Bucs line up in a bear front, and stunt the play side 3 tech into the A gap. The over hang falls into the B gap, but the wideout does a nice job of digging him out. The corner in man coverage on the wideout comes off and makes a nice tackle short of the first down.

With no second fall back from the Vikings inside linebacker in the divisional round, the cutback lane is large. The running back does not have a chance to get to the cutback lane, however.

As the RB is trying to make a cut in week 10, he gets tripped by his front side guard who is getting blown back by the play side 3 tech. Once again, there is a nice cutback to be had on this play.

Outside Zone – Strong - Slice

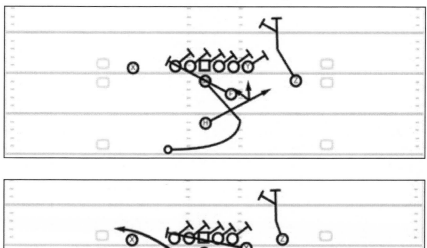

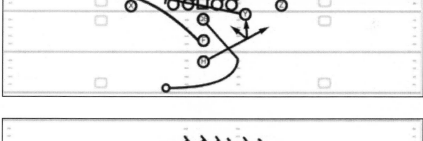

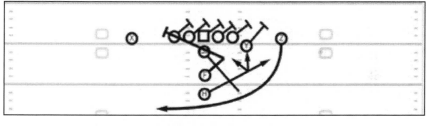

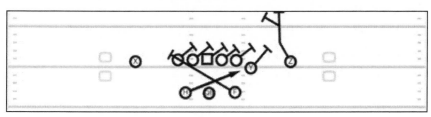

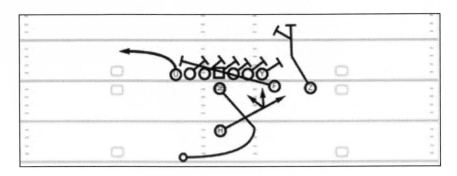

Average Yards per Play	8.8

1st Down		3rd/4th Down (includes RZ)	
Called	Average	Called	Success Rate
9	9.0	0	0%
2nd Down 6-1		2nd Down 7+	
Called	Average	Called	Average
3	8.7	1	8.0
Red Zone 10-0		Red Zone 10-20	
Called	Touchdown %	Called	Touchdown %
1	0%	1	0%

Bear		Over	
Called	Average	Called	Average
2	1.5	8	12.1
Under		Mug	
Called	Average	Called	Average
3	5.0	0	0.0
Wide		Odd	
Called	Average	Called	Average
0	0.0	0	0.0

Week	Quarter	Time	Down	ToGo	Location	Yards
Week 13 vs BAL	2	9:22	1	10	RAV 40	40
Week 13 vs BAL	3	11:26	2	6	SFO 24	18
Week 13 vs BAL	3	10:19	2	1	RAV 49	1
DIV vs MIN	1	10:55	1	10	MIN 16	2
DIV vs MIN	2	4:45	1	10	SFO 8	1
DIV vs MIN	2	4:06	2	9	SFO 9	8
DIV vs MIN	3	13:42	1	10	MIN 37	5
DIV vs MIN	3	7:47	2	4	MIN 28	7
DIV vs MIN	3	1:05	1	10	MIN 10	2
DIV vs MIN	4	12:42	1	10	SFO 14	2
NFCCG vs GB	1	15:00	1	10	SFO 25	5
SB vs KC	1	11:51	1	10	KAN 40	7
SB vs KC	2	6:41	1	10	KAN 43	17

Outside of the DIV vs MIN game, the 49ers seldom used this concept.

Why it Worked: In week 13, the "Z" receiver is able to dig out the DB playing the C gap, and the play hits front side C gap for a big play TD.

The 49ers used the version in the 2nd diagram for their big run in the Super Bowl. They get the DE, rolled down safety, and inside linebacker to fall out of the box for the slice and arrow. They get a "3 for 2". The right guard is able to reach the back side 1 tech without the center's help because of the quick snap count.

Why it Didn't Work: The last clip in week 13, the Z is not able to dig out the safety playing the C gap and he makes the tackle for a short gain.

Outside Zone – Weak - Slice

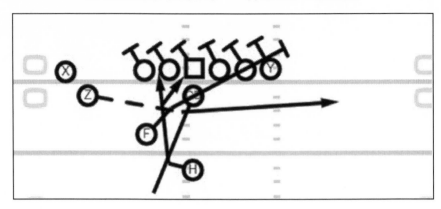

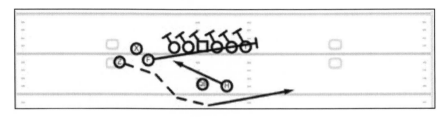

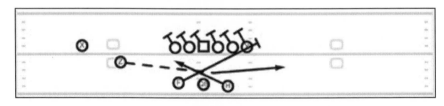

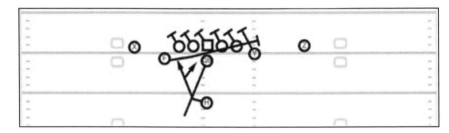

Average Yards per Play	7.8

1st Down		3rd/4th Down (includes RZ)	
Called	Average	Called	Success Rate
4	4.5	0	0%
2nd Down 6-1		**2nd Down 7+**	
Called	Average	Called	Average
2	4.0	2	18.0
Red Zone 10-0		**Red Zone 10-20**	
Called	Touchdown %	Called	Touchdown %
0	0%	0	0%

Bear		Over	
Called	Average	Called	Average
1	-1.0	6	9.5
Under		**Mug**	
Called	Average	Called	Average
0	0.0	0	0.0
Wide		**Odd**	
Called	Average	Called	Average
0	0.0	1	6.0

Week	Quarter	Time	Down	ToGo	Location	Yards
Week 8 vs CAR	1	12:29	1	10	SFO 48	11
Week 8 vs CAR	1	4:23	1	10	SFO 25	-1
Week 8 vs CAR	2	3:12	2	6	SFO 41	2
Week 10 vs SEA	1	14:19	2	9	SFO 26	-1
Week 15 vs ATL	2	2:31	2	15	SFO 20	37
DIV vs MIN	1	13:41	1	10	SFO 39	2
DIV vs MIN	3	9:09	2	6	MIN 40	6
DIV vs MIN	3	8:27	1	10	MIN 34	6

While used sparingly, this concept was still a part of the outside zone arsenal.

The intricacies of the play are similar to "Inside Zone – Weak – Slice". This section goes into more detail about the concept.

This version is designed to hit the cutback. With the fake jet/comet motion, the defense has to "fall back" twice.

Why it Worked: Even though the play is not blocked up perfectly in week 15, the cutback lane is still large enough for the 49ers to rip off a big gain.

Why it Didn't Work: In week 8, the backside 3 technique blows up the backside tackle.

Outside Zone – 10 Personnel and RPO's

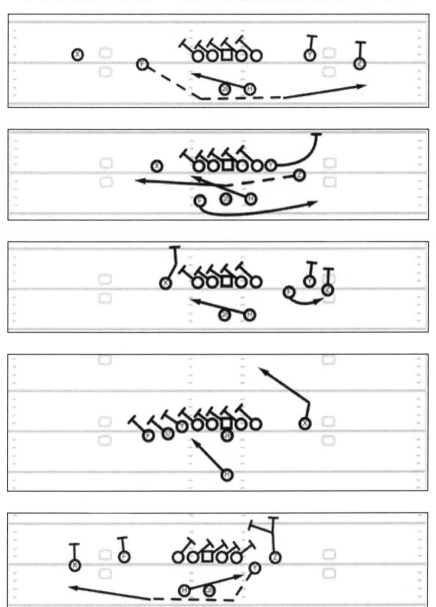

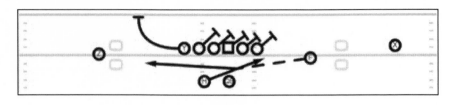

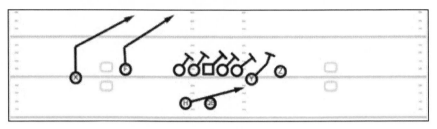

Average Yards per Play	7.3

1st Down		3rd/4th Down (includes RZ)	
Called	Average	Called	Success Rate
4	9.0	1	0%
2nd Down 6-1		2nd Down 7+	
Called	Average	Called	Average
1	0.0	5	8.6
Red Zone 10-0		Red Zone 10-20	
Called	Touchdown %	Called	Touchdown %
2	0%	1	0%

Bear		Over	
Called	Average	Called	Average
1	12.0	9	7.4
Under		Mug	
Called	Average	Called	Average
1	1.0	0	0.0
Wide		Odd	
Called	Average	Called	Average
0	0.0	0	0.0

Week	Quarter	Time	Down	ToGo	Location	Yards
Week 8 vs CAR	3	8:02	2	6	CAR 28	0
Week 8 vs CAR	4	13:39	3	3	CAR 3	1
Week 10 vs SEA	2	1:00	2	7	SFO 5	17
Week 15 vs ATL	1	5:51	1	10	SFO 45	8
Week 15 vs ATL	3	14:51	1	10	SFO 31	12
Week 17 vs SEA	3	4:46	2	9	SEA 25	24
DIV vs MIN	3	0:29	2	8	MIN 8	4
NFCCG vs GB	2	2:13	2	8	GNB 15	0
SB vs KC	1	8:57	2	8	KAN 23	-2
SB vs KC	2	5:55	1	10	KAN 26	11
SB vs KC	3	11:59	1	10	KAN 32	5

With all of the variation in the 49ers run game, they create hesitation in defensive ends enough to where they can leave them unblocked and still run an RPO without getting the quarterback blown up. The hesitation leaves him in no man's land and gives the offense a +1 for the run call, getting the backside tackle involved on the front side instead of "locking" him on the end.

The 4th diagram shows a 13 personnel formation RPO. The Seahawks loaded the line of scrimmage with 6 defenders in week 17, so the slant had no inside help.

Why it Worked: Garoppolo hit the slant in week 17. In week 10, the Seahawks rotate a safety into the box late, leaving the bubble side with a 3 on 2 in favor of the offense.

Why it Didn't Work: In the Super Bowl, the bubble screen gets blown up. The box numbers and post snap safety rotation favored the handoff here.

Outside Zone – BS Lock (With RPO's)

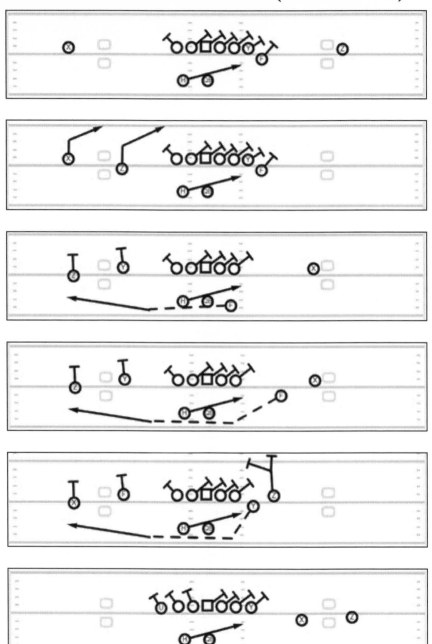

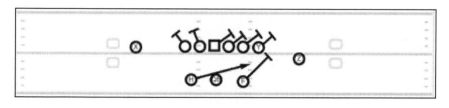

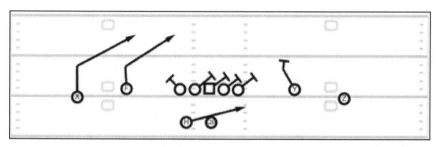

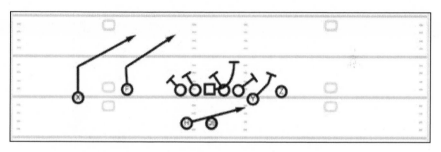

Average Yards per Play	6.3

1st Down		3rd/4th Down (includes RZ)	
Called	Average	Called	Success Rate
13	4.3	1	0%
2nd Down 6-1		**2nd Down 7+**	
Called	Average	Called	Average
3	2.3	5	14.0
Red Zone 10-0		**Red Zone 10-20**	
Called	Touchdown %	Called	Touchdown %
1	0%	2	50%

Week	Quarter	Time	Down	ToGo	Location	Yards
Week 2 vs CIN	3	5:28	2	14	CIN 32	12
Week 2 vs CIN	4	3:00	3	9	SFO 27	6
Week 3 vs PIT	1	8:16	2	28	SFO 31	13
Week 3 vs PIT	1	1:59	1	10	SFO 31	2
Week 6 vs LA	3	9:21	1	10	RAM 39	3
Week 6 vs LA	4	9:34	2	4	RAM 39	-1
Week 8 vs CAR	1	11:49	2	10	CAR 41	22
Week 8 vs CAR	1	1:15	2	11	CAR 19	19
Week 8 vs CAR	2	13:21	1	10	CAR 10	0
Week 9 vs ARI	3	14:55	1	10	SFO 28	0
Week 10 vs SEA	1	12:16	2	10	SEA 49	4
Week 11 vs ARI	4	14:30	1	10	CRD 18	0
Week 13 vs BAL	1	13:01	1	10	RAV 41	8
Week 13 vs BAL	1	8:57	1	10	SFO 16	2
Week 13 vs BAL	4	14:20	1	10	SFO 32	-3
Week 14 vs NO	2	2:00	1	10	NOR 32	7
Week 16 vs LAR	1	6:59	1	10	SFO 35	4
Week 16 vs LAR	1	6:25	2	6	SFO 39	1
DIV vs MIN	3	13:04	2	5	MIN 32	7
NFCCG vs GB	2	1:01	1	10	GNB 30	11
NFCCG vs GB	4	7:24	1	10	SFO 46	5
SB vs KC	4	2:39	1	10	SFO 15	17

Bear		Over	
Called	Average	Called	Average
0	0.0	14	6.9
Under		**Mug**	
Called	Average	Called	Average
8	5.4	0	0.0
Wide		**Odd**	
Called	Average	Called	Average
0	0.0	0	0.0

The lock rules are simple. The backside tackle will always lock on the 5 technique. The back side guard will lock on a 3technique, if present. The following diagrams show each version.

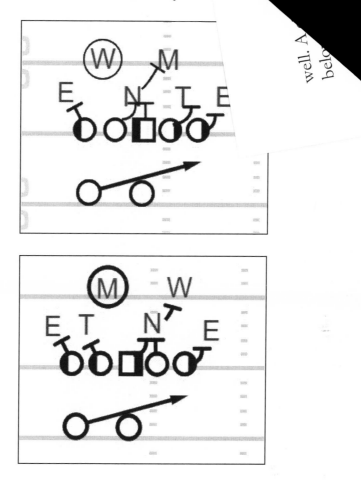

The play was not called against an odd front.

The big benefit of locking the backside on outside zone is the offense does not have to worry about backside penetration, specifically from a 3 technique. When the 3 technique is on the front side, the attached RPO is a great way to take advantage of the back side linebackers pursuit. Attaching slants on the backside is a great way to attack that void left by the vacating linebacker. A good clip of this can be seen in week 3.

With a 1 technique play side, a fold call can be made as

clip of this can be seen in week 3. The diagram
w shows the fold call.

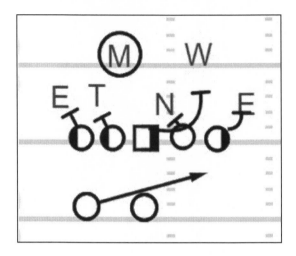

The 5th diagram shows a unique variation that gets the
tight end on an orbit bubble screen. This is a great way to
get athletic do-it-all tight end George Kittle in space. This
clip can be seen in week 3.

The 49ers would also occasionally leave the 3 technique
unblocked in their lock scheme. The TD in week 8 shows a
great clip of this. The play is shown below.

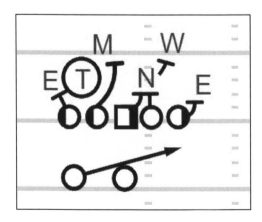

In week 16, the also left the 3 technique unblocked, but they sliced him with the fullback. This play is shown below.

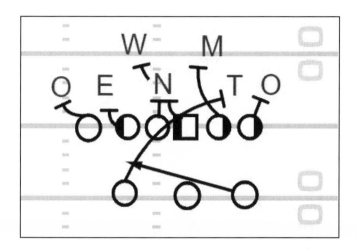

Why it Worked: In general, this play can be effective with strong interior line play and a QB who can read the back side linebacker.

In week 14, Mostert showed excellent patience and vision to rip off a big play.

Garoppolo pulls the ball and throws the slant in week 3 for a nice gain.

The 22 yard touchdown in week 8 shows the variation with the 3 technique unblocked.

Why it Didn't Work: In week 9, Garoppolo gets a pull read, but the Cardinals doe a nice job pressing the slants from inside leverage. In week 13, the tight end does not pick up a run through linebacker on the front side.

Outside Zone Strong – 2 TE's Front Side

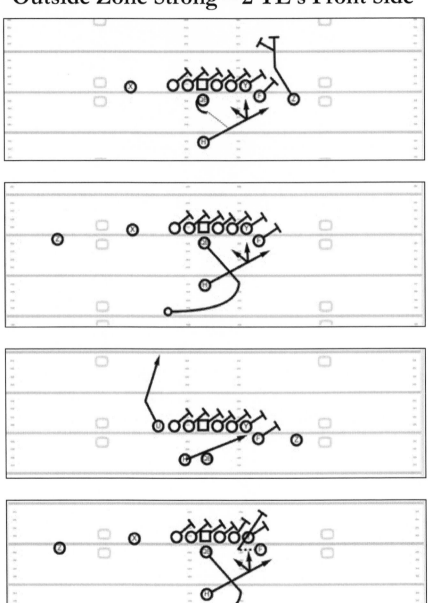

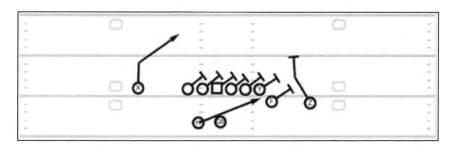

Average Yards per Play	5.3

1st Down		3rd/4th Down (includes RZ)	
Called	Average	Called	Success Rate
11	4.9	0	0%
2nd Down 6-1		**2nd Down 7+**	
Called	Average	Called	Average
2	0.0	5	8.2
Red Zone 10-0		**Red Zone 10-20**	
Called	Touchdown %	Called	Touchdown %
0	0%	0	0%

Bear		Over	
Called	Average	Called	Average
1	30.0	7	3.7
Under		**Mug**	
Called	Average	Called	Average
8	3.4	0	0.0
Wide		**Odd**	
Called	Average	Called	Average
0	0.0	2	6.0

Week	Quarter	Time	Down	ToGo	Location	Yards
Week 5 vs CLE	2	11:18	2	10	SFO 25	15
Week 5 vs CLE	4	9:04	2	14	SFO 22	-4
Week 6 vs LA	1	7:56	2	10	SFO 36	2
Week 6 vs LA	3	3:41	1	10	SFO 42	7
Week 6 vs LA	4	14:15	1	10	RAM 24	0
Week 6 vs LA	**4**	**9:34**	**2**	**4**	**RAM 39**	**-1**
Week 6 vs LA	4	2:19	1	10	RAM 46	0
Week 7 vs WAS	2	4:02	1	10	SFO 29	9
Week 7 vs WAS	3	1:20	1	10	SFO 41	3
Week 8 vs CAR	**1**	**11:49**	**2**	**10**	**CAR 41**	**22**
Week 8 vs CAR	1	3:11	1	10	SFO 36	2
Week 9 vs ARI	**3**	**14:55**	**1**	**10**	**SFO 28**	**0**
Week 10 vs SEA	1	6:17	1	10	SFO 17	30
Week 13 vs BAL	**1**	**8:57**	**1**	**10**	**SFO 16**	**2**
Week 13 vs BAL	**4**	**14:20**	**1**	**10**	**SFO 32**	**-3**
Week 14 vs NO	3	12:00	2	7	SFO 28	6
Week 16 vs LAR	**1**	**6:25**	**2**	**6**	**SFO 39**	**1**
NFCCG vs GB	1	1:29	1	10	GNB 32	4

This variation of outside zone is used to pop the play outside. The two tight end surface gives the offense leverage to outflank the defense.

The plays that are bolded have the backside "locked".

If the defense wants to line up outside of the 2nd TE, the first cutback lane is larger than it typically would be based on alignment.

Why it Worked : The big plays come when the ball gets to the edge with this version of outside zone. That was the case for the big runs.

The slant RPO was hit for a big play in week 10.

Why it Didn't Work : The front side 3 tech dips inside to blow it up in week 5. Luke Kuechly gets off the front side tackles block to make a play in week 8.

Inside Zone – Weak - Slice – 11/21/12/22 Personnel

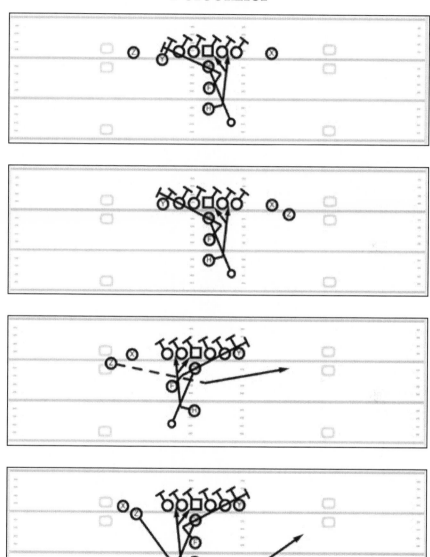

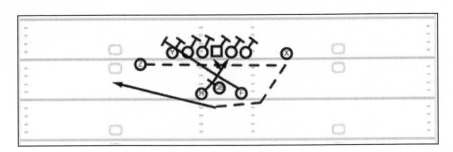

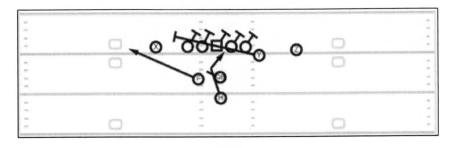

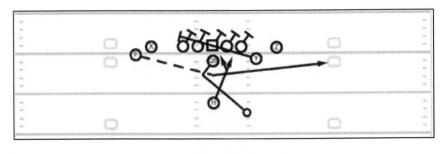

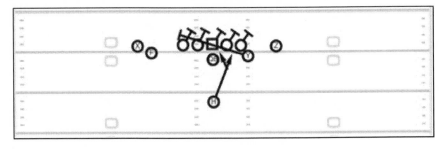

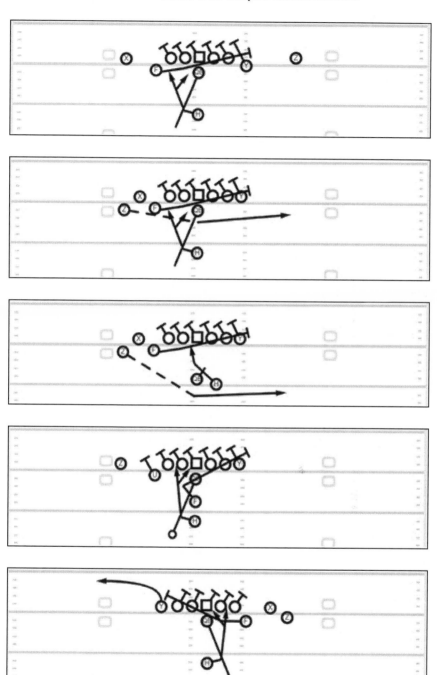

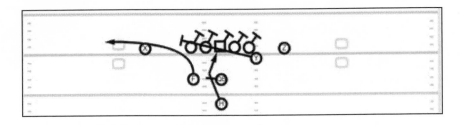

Average Yards per Play	5.7

1st Down		3rd/4th Down (includes RZ)	
Called	Average	Called	Success Rate
31	6.7	2	50%
2nd Down 6-1		**2nd Down 7+**	
Called	Average	Called	Average
3	2.0	6	3.0
Red Zone 10-0		**Red Zone 10-20**	
Called	Touchdown %	Called	Touchdown %
3	33%	3	33%

Bear		Over	
Called	Average	Called	Average
9	5.6	18	7.9
Under		**Mug**	
Called	Average	Called	Average
10	3.0	0	0.0
Wide		**Odd**	
Called	Average	Called	Average
0	0.0	4	4.3

Week	Quarter	Time	Down	ToGo	Location	Yards
Week 1 vs TB	1	13:28	1	10	TAM 33	1
Week 1 vs TB	2	9:48	1	10	SFO 20	1
Week 1 vs TB	2	5:26	2	3	TAM 24	0
Week 1 vs TB	3	13:17	1	10	TAM 40	1
Week 1 vs TB	4	9:06	3	18	SFO 4	0
Week 3 vs PIT	1	5:28	1	10	SFO 28	-1
Week 3 vs PIT	3	3:46	1	10	PIT 44	5
Week 3 vs PIT	3	1:02	1	4	PIT 4	4
Week 5 vs CLE	1	13:28	1	10	SFO 17	83
Week 5 vs CLE	1	7:06	2	9	CLE 9	4
Week 5 vs CLE	3	11:21	1	10	CLE 23	1
Week 5 vs CLE	3	7:17	1	10	SFO 32	6
Week 5 vs CLE	3	3:45	1	10	CLE 42	3
Week 5 vs CLE	4	9:46	1	10	SFO 26	0
Week 7 vs WAS	3	15:00	1	10	SFO 25	3
Week 7 vs WAS	3	9:22	2	8	SFO 25	5
Week 7 vs WAS	4	2:00	2	10	WAS 16	-1
Week 8 vs CAR	3	8:45	1	10	CAR 32	4
Week 8 vs CAR	3	5:56	1	10	CAR 45	0
Week 8 vs CAR	4	2:44	3	4	CAR 35	6
Week 10 vs SEA	1	5:38	1	5	SEA 48	22
Week 10 vs SEA	2	3:38	1	10	SFO 20	3
Week 10 vs SEA	2	2:51	1	10	SFO 25	1
Week 11 vs ARI	1	3:23	2	7	CRD 42	2
Week 11 vs ARI	3	11:48	1	3	CRD 3	-2
Week 12 vs GB	2	4:52	1	10	GNB 28	11
Week 12 vs GB	4	10:46	2	12	SFO 29	2
Week 12 vs GB	4	7:13	1	10	GNB 28	5
Week 12 vs GB	4	5:04	1	10	GNB 15	15
Week 13 vs BAL	4	8:36	1	10	RAV 44	3
Week 14 vs NO	1	4:51	1	10	SFO 25	1
Week 14 vs NO	4	5:22	2	5	SFO 30	3
Week 14 vs NO	4	2:45	1	10	NOR 24	5
Week 16 vs LAR	3	12:44	1	10	RAM 44	5
Week 16 vs LAR	4	8:05	1	10	SFO 45	12
Week 17 vs SEA	1	9:15	1	10	SEA 28	1
DIV vs MIN	3	14:56	1	10	SFO 37	5
DIV vs MIN	3	9:49	1	10	MIN 44	4
NFCCG vs GB	2	9:44	1	10	GNB 13	4
NFCCG vs GB	4	13:52	2	6	GNB 44	3
NFCCG vs GB	4	5:08	2	8	GNB 29	6
SB vs KC	3	4:42	1	10	KAN 39	2

When running 21/12 personnel inside zone weak with the slice block, there are a few rules to clean up the picture on the back side for the tight end and fullback. If the OLB is walked up (typically in an under front), the tight end will bluff him, and get up on the inside linebacker if the defensive end is in a 6i/5 technique. The fullback will take the first man outside the tackle, the defensive end. This adjustment works nice with the fake jet motion going to the tight end, as it will hold the Sam as well. The image below shows the adjustment.

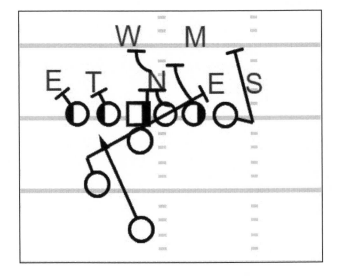

The next diagram shows the same adjustment made against an over front with a 6 technique on the tight end.

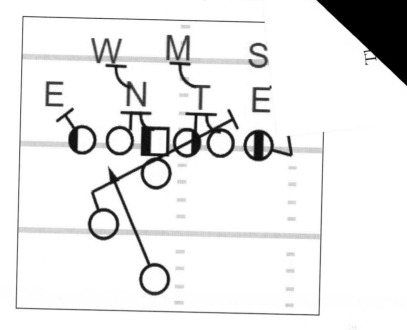

This action typically creates a nice cutback lane for the back to hit backside C gap. The arcing tight end will block the player "falling back" for the slice action.

With a head up 4 technique defensive end, the tight end will combo down with the tackle. The play is shown below.

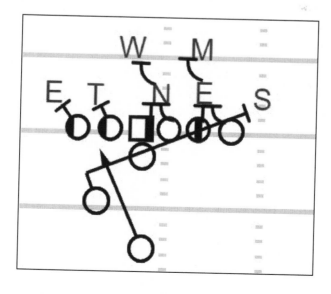

here are even a few clips where it looks like the cutback was intended. These were the 21/22 personnel variations with the fullback selling the lead action to the front side first.

The variation with the slice block going to the tight end led to a few big cutback lanes for big plays. The first play of the game against Cleveland

The 7th diagram shows a variation with the fake jet motion going towards the side the line is blocking inside zone to. In this variation, the fake jet motion acts as a misdirection for the fall back, forcing the defense to bump one way, and fall back to their original spots. To seal the game on a 3rd and 4 in week 8, this variation was called. The bump from the fake jet motion distracts the back side inside linebacker from "falling back" into his backside B gap responsibility, leaving the cutback desired for this concept.

Why it Worked: In week 12, the 49ers hit this concept for a 15 yard touchdown. They get an awesome combo up to the linebacker from the tight end and backside tackle.

For the 12 yard gainer in week 16, Juszczyk takes an awesome path and seals the D gap player. The back side tackle does a nice job 1 on 1 with his guy, creating a nice cutback lane.

Why it Didn't Work: In week 10, the Seahawks showed how stunting the defensive front can give zone blocking schemes problems. The front side 5 technique slips inside the play side tackle to get into the backfield quickly.

In week 1, Kittle tries to down block on the 5 technique. This didn't go so well. This game might have been the point where the 49ers coaching staff decided to have the TE arc 5 techniques for the remainder of the season.

Inside Zone – Strong - Slice 21/12/22 Personnel

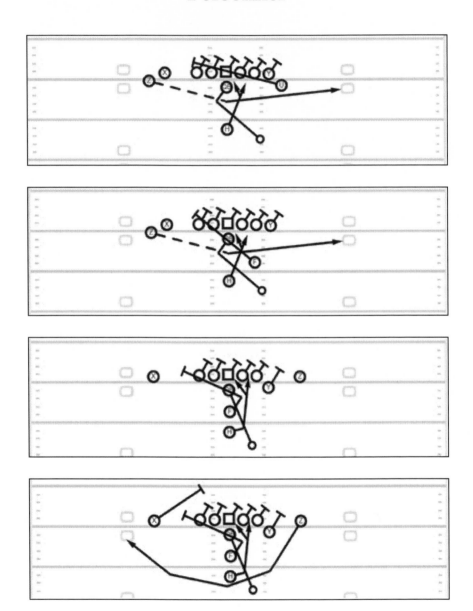

Average Yards per Play	4.5

1st Down		3rd/4th Down (includes RZ)	
Called	Average	Called	Success Rate
13	3.8	0	0%
2nd Down 6-1		2nd Down 7+	
Called	Average	Called	Average
2	6.0	2	7.5
Red Zone 10-0		Red Zone 10-20	
Called	Touchdown %	Called	Touchdown %
0	0%	1	0%

Week	Quarter	Time	Down	ToGo	Location	Yards
Week 2 vs CIN	2	12:50	1	10	SFO 42	4
Week 2 vs CIN	4	10:44	2	9	CIN 31	6
Week 5 vs CLE	3	13:49	1	10	SFO 30	4
Week 5 vs CLE	4	14:46	1	10	SFO 22	0
Week 12 vs GB	2	4:52	1	10	GNB 28	11
Week 12 vs GB	4	7:13	1	10	GNB 28	5
Week 12 vs GB	4	6:26	2	5	GNB 23	3
Week 15 vs ATL	1	6:27	2	2	SFO 36	9
Week 15 vs ATL	3	8:50	1	10	ATL 48	8
Week 15 vs ATL	3	0:44	1	10	ATL 38	4
Week 15 vs ATL	4	2:48	1	10	ATL 34	2
Week 17 vs SEA	2	10:45	1	10	SFO 36	2
Week 17 vs SEA	2	9:28	2	10	SEA 47	9
Week 17 vs SEA	4	3:35	1	10	SFO 21	3
DIV vs MIN	1	4:05	1	10	SFO 35	3
NFCCG vs GB	2	2:54	1	10	GNB 17	2
SB vs KC	2	9:26	1	10	SFO 20	1

Bear		Over	
Called	Average	Called	Average
0	0.0	8	4.0
Under		Mug	
Called	Average	Called	Average
9	4.9	0	0.0
Wide		Odd	
Called	Average	Called	Average
0	0.0	0	0.0

This variation was used much less that the Weak – Slice version.

The play was primarily called on first downs.

The last diagram shows a variation with a crack block that was used in week 15 a couple times. The crack block will pin the new C gap player inside.

Why it Worked: The crack version worked for a few nice runs in week 15. The ghost action kept the corner wide, and allowed the back to bounce it outside the slice block and inside the corner.

Why it Didn't Work: Interior push from the defensive line slowed the play up a couple of times. In general, the 49ers gained positive yards each time it was called in 2019.

Inside Zone - Weak

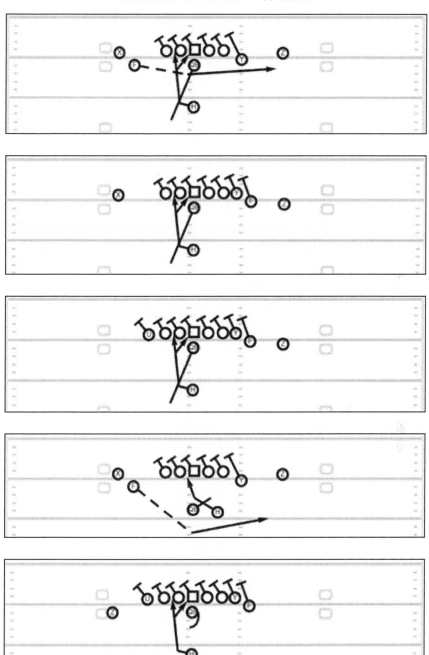

Average Yards per Play	5.3

1st Down		3rd/4th Down (includes RZ)	
Called	Average	Called	Success Rate
5	1.4	2	50%
2nd Down 6-1		**2nd Down 7+**	
Called	Average	Called	Average
2	5.5	1	0.0
Red Zone 10-0		**Red Zone 10-20**	
Called	Touchdown %	Called	Touchdown %
3	33%	0	0%

Bear		Over	
Called	Average	Called	Average
4	11.8	4	0.8
Under		**Mug**	
Called	Average	Called	Average
1	1.0	0	0.0
Wide		**Odd**	
Called	Average	Called	Average
0	0.0	0	0.0

Week	Quarter	Time	Down	ToGo	Location	Yards
Week 2 vs CIN	1	5:57	1	10	SFO 30	3
Week 2 vs CIN	2	11:26	3	1	CIN 49	34
Week 2 vs CIN	2	10:48	2	1	CIN 6	4
Week 2 vs CIN	3	1:55	2	4	CIN 40	7
Week 5 vs CLE	2	4:16	1	10	CLE 36	1
Week 6 vs LA	3	14:05	1	3	RAM 3	2
Week 6 vs LA	4	4:24	2	8	SFO 44	0
Week 9 vs ARI	4	9:19	1	10	SFO 17	-1
Week 10 vs SEA	OT	3:26	3	2	SEA 30	1
Week 15 vs ATL	2	12:59	1	2	ATL 2	2

Inside zone weak is a staple version of inside zone in most spread offenses. It has its place as a change of pace in Shanahan's offense.

Most of the time when it is called, inside zone will cutback just behind the center. Using a tight end on the weak side will ensure that the end is capped for the running back. This play is a downhill run, and frequently used in short yardage situations.

Faking the jet sweep with this action will hold the second level defenders for a second and allow the double teams to work longer.

Why it Worked: Matt Breida's excellent run in week 2 came on a third and 1. The Bengals plugged up the front, and Breida bounced it weak to the outside. He had quite a few cuts, making defenders miss along the way.

The 4th down conversion in week 6 was a zone read variation. Garoppolo pulled the ball to pick up the first down.

Why it Didn't Work: In week 9, the stand up outside linebacker shot under the tight end to catch the play from behind.

Inside Zone – Lead – Weak (& Lock Tag)

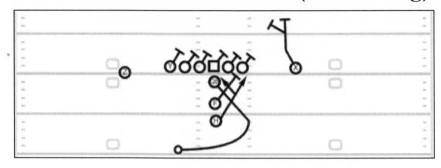

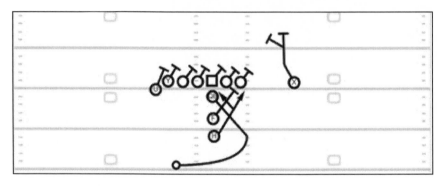

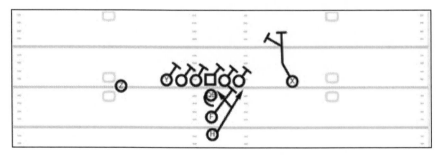

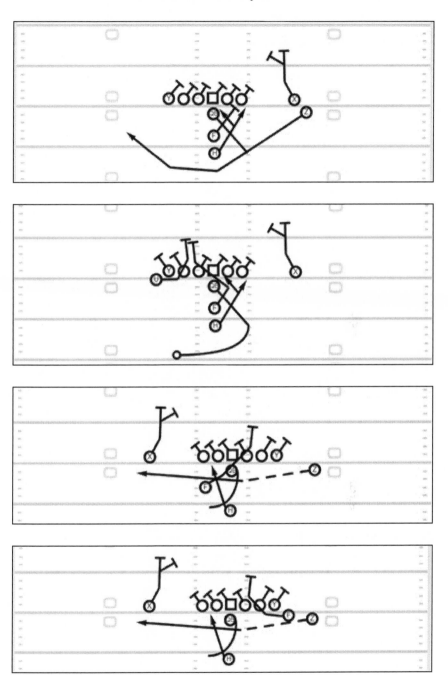

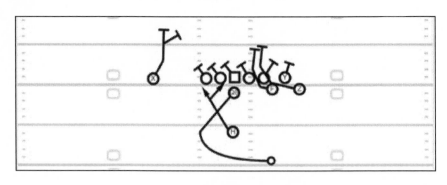

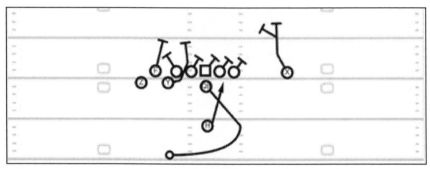

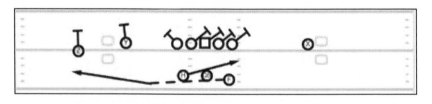

Average Yards per Play	4.3

1st Down		3rd/4th Down (includes RZ)	
Called	Average	Called	Success Rate
17	4.6	2	50%
2nd Down 6-1		2nd Down 7+	
Called	Average	Called	Average
9	4.4	1	4.0
Red Zone 10-0		Red Zone 10-20	
Called	Touchdown %	Called	Touchdown %
5	0%	3	0%

Bear		Over	
Called	Average	Called	Average
6	3.2	3	7.3
Under		**Mug**	
Called	Average	Called	Average
9	5.0	0	0.0
Wide		**Odd**	
Called	Average	Called	Average
0	0.0	9	3.2

Week	Quarter	Time	Down	ToGo	Location	Yards
Week 1 vs TB	3	4:05	2	2	TAM 44	5
Week 1 vs TB	4	10:51	1	15	SFO 7	0
Week 1 vs TB	4	3:22	1	10	SFO 36	18
Week 1 vs TB	4	3:12	1	10	TAM 31	0
Week 2 vs CIN	2	12:07	2	6	SFO 46	5
Week 2 vs CIN	3	1:10	1	10	CIN 33	20
Week 2 vs CIN	4	9:17	1	10	CIN 15	-6
Week 3 vs PIT	1	0:44	1	10	PIT 28	3
Week 3 vs PIT	3	13:19	1	10	PIT 38	5
Week 3 vs PIT	3	12:01	1	10	PIT 27	2
Week 3 vs PIT	3	5:15	2	1	SFO 34	0
Week 3 vs PIT	3	3:10	2	5	PIT 39	10
Week 3 vs PIT	3	2:17	1	10	PIT 18	2
Week 3 vs PIT	4	8:11	2	4	PIT 13	5
Week 3 vs PIT	4	7:44	1	8	PIT 8	1
Week 6 vs LA	1	0:34	2	8	SFO 40	4
Week 6 vs LA	3	2:18	1	10	RAM 47	2
Week 7 vs WAS	1	6:46	1	10	SFO 29	1
Week 7 vs WAS	2	15:00	3	6	WAS 36	6
Week 8 vs CAR	3	13:24	1	10	SFO 2	3
Week 8 vs CAR	4	15:00	1	9	CAR 9	4
Week 8 vs CAR	4	14:24	2	5	CAR 5	2
Week 9 vs ARI	3	2:24	1	10	CRD 46	-3
Week 11 vs ARI	3	13:28	2	1	CRD 23	6
Week 14 vs NO	2	2:31	1	10	SFO 40	28
Week 14 vs NO	3	11:18	3	1	SFO 34	-3
Week 15 vs ATL	2	1:07	2	3	ATL 3	-1
Week 15 vs ATL	4	4:29	2	6	SFO 29	8
Week 17 vs SEA	3	4:04	1	1	SEA 1	-1

This version of inside zone seems to hit best when run into an over or under front. With a bubble in either the A gap or B gap, the lead blocker will have an easy time of finding where to lead through. Out of 21 personnel, the offense won't see as much true over front, so it will typically be the A gap vs the under front. A good clip of this can be seen in week 11. The play is shown below.

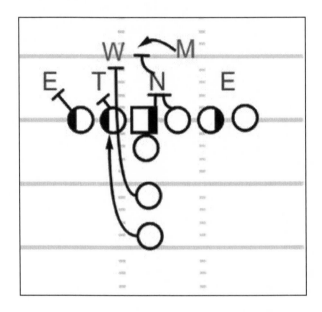

The variations with a "lock" tag are bolded. The "lock" rules are the same as described in "Outside Zone – BS Lock (with RPO's)" section. The lead blocker will insert into the split where the line starts to lock. The 49ers were more successful with the "lock" variations, doubling their yards per carry.

The fifth diagram shows a 22 personnel variation with a double insert used in week 1. The 10th diagram shows the lock insert version that hit big in week 14.

Why it Worked: The 28 yard gainer in week 14 was executed perfectly. The Saints play an Under G front. Kittle inserts into the B gap, and helps the guard with the 2i. Bourne comes down and digs out the linebacker that follows Kittle.

The lead version hit for a big run in week 1 when the 49ers were trying to put Tampa away. The play hits the open weak B gap in an over front. Although the front side combo isn't perfect, Mostert hits the Mike with a nice stiff arm to break into the third level.

Why it Didn't Work: In week 9, the Cardinals stunt the 5 technique across the front side tackle's face and bring a guy off the edge. The tackle takes the 5 tech, and the edge player is unblocked. This is another example of how line movement can give offenses problems on zone schemes.

Power

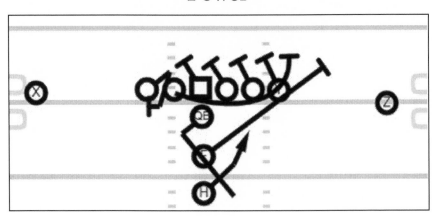

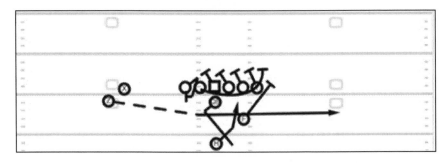

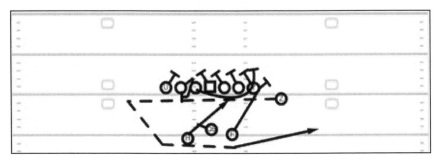

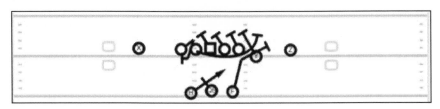

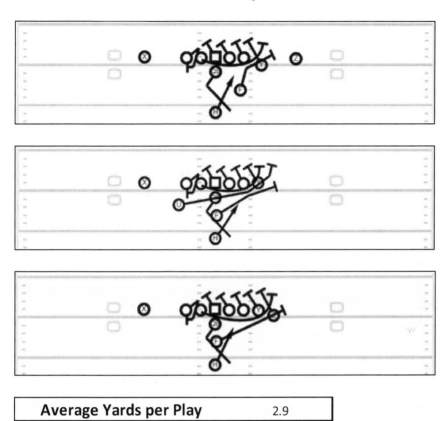

Average Yards per Play	2.9

1st Down		3rd/4th Down (includes RZ)	
Called	Average	Called	Success Rate
15	1.9	5	75%
2nd Down 6-1		2nd Down 7+	
Called	Average	Called	Average
5	2.0	2	5.0
Red Zone 10-0		Red Zone 10-20	
Called	Touchdown %	Called	Touchdown %
3	67%	5	0%

Bear		Over	
Called	Average	Called	Average
7	1.9	4	2.5
Under		**Mug**	
Called	Average	Called	Average
12	3.2	0	0.0
Wide		**Odd**	
Called	Average	Called	Average
1	2.0	1	2.0

Week	Quarter	Time	Down	ToGo	Location	Yards
Week 2 vs CIN	4	15:00	2	1	CIN 4	4
Week 5 vs CLE	2	2:05	4	1	CLE 27	8
Week 5 vs CLE	3	9:08	1	10	SFO 4	2
Week 7 vs WAS	2	13:38	2	3	WAS 23	2
Week 8 vs CAR	1	9:53	1	2	CAR 2	-2
Week 9 vs ARI	1	3:55	2	1	SFO 50	2
Week 9 vs ARI	4	3:54	1	10	SFO 41	5
Week 9 vs ARI	4	3:11	2	5	SFO 46	2
Week 9 vs ARI	4	2:17	2	12	SFO 49	8
Week 10 vs SEA	2	10:07	2	10	SFO 27	2
Week 11 vs ARI	1	1:13	1	10	SFO 15	-1
Week 11 vs ARI	2	2:00	1	10	CRD 34	4
Week 11 vs ARI	3	7:10	1	10	CRD 17	2
Week 11 vs ARI	4	0:25	1	10	CRD 30	2
Week 11 vs ARI	4	0:16	3	4	CRD 24	3
Week 12 vs GB	4	5:47	3	2	GNB 20	5
Week 13 vs BAL	3	1:31	1	10	SFO 1	3
Week 14 vs NO	4	0:28	1	10	NOR 14	3
Week 17 vs SEA	3	5:25	1	10	SEA 26	1
DIV vs MIN	3	5:39	3	2	MIN 13	11
DIV vs MIN	3	4:57	1	2	MIN 2	2
NFCCG vs GB	2	11:04	2	1	GNB 15	0
NFCCG vs GB	3	6:41	1	10	SFO 44	2
NFCCG vs GB	4	5:53	1	10	GNB 42	-1
NFCCG vs GB	4	5:23	3	1	GNB 33	2
SB vs KC	4	11:57	1	10	SFO 20	6
SB vs KC	4	10:37	1	10	SFO 38	1

The power scheme is an important piece in the 49ers vast run game menu. The play gives the 49ers an "attitude" run out of their 21/22 personnel sets.

With a lead late in games, the 49ers liked to use the power scheme to salt away the clock.

Power is typically preferred to the 3 technique side. The front side guard and tackle will work a double team on the 3 technique, up to the back side linebacker. This is drawn up in the next section, Power (1 Back).

 When the 49ers played heavy under front teams, they would motion the tight end to get the defense to set the strength one way, then run power to the original weak side where the 3 technique is lined up. A clip of this can be seen in week 9 4Q 3:54.

Power was a popular call in both matchups with the Arizona Cardinals.

The third diagram shows the 4th and 1 call in week 5.

The sixth diagram shows a 22 personnel version with two pullers used in 1Q week 11.

Why it Worked: With the Browns playing a goal line front on 4th 1 in week 5, the 49ers were able to wash down the front side of the line and make a nice hole for a big gain. In week 12, the 49ers used tempo out of the huddle and the Packers were not set

Why it Didn't Work: In week 11, the Cardinals brought a safety off the front side edge. The play side TE and both pullers missed the safety. In week 8, the safety shot through the play side A gap in the low red zone.

Power (1 Back)

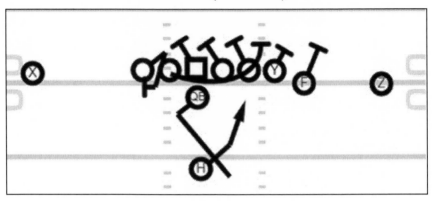

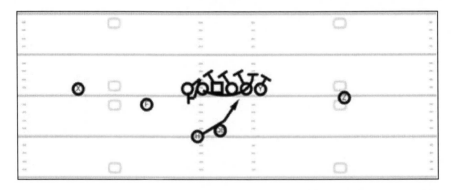

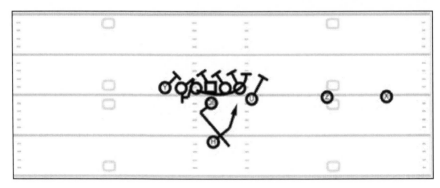

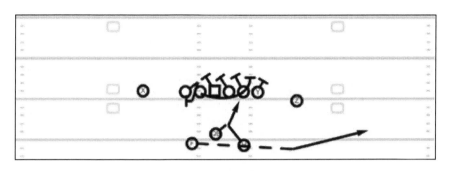

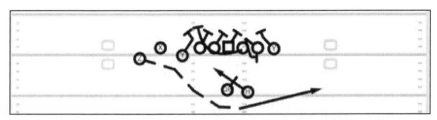

Average Yards per Play	4.6

1st Down		3rd/4th Down (includes RZ)	
Called	Average	Called	Success Rate
7	3.6	3	33%
2nd Down 6-1		**2nd Down 7+**	
Called	Average	Called	Average
2	3.0	4	3.5
Red Zone 10-0		**Red Zone 10-20**	
Called	Touchdown %	Called	Touchdown %
2	50%	3	33%

Bear		Over	
Called	Average	Called	Average
1	0.0	7	4.4
Under		**Mug**	
Called	Average	Called	Average
4	6.8	0	0.0
Wide		**Odd**	
Called	Average	Called	Average
1	10.0	2	2.0

Week	Quarter	Time	Down	ToGo	Location	Yards
Week 2 vs CIN	4	3:10	2	12	SFO 24	3
Week 3 vs PIT	2	7:28	3	15	PIT 16	10
Week 3 vs PIT	2	0:05	2	15	SFO 15	5
Week 3 vs PIT	4	12:08	3	23	SFO 12	10
Week 6 vs LA	3	2:58	2	3	SFO 49	4
Week 6 vs LA	4	15:00	2	1	RAM 26	2
Week 6 vs LA	4	7:34	1	10	SFO 28	0
Week 6 vs LA	4	2:00	2	10	RAM 46	4
Week 6 vs LA	4	1:55	3	6	RAM 42	8
Week 8 vs CAR	3	1:50	1	10	CAR 10	1
Week 13 vs BAL	1	14:54	1	10	SFO 26	0
Week 16 vs LAR	4	0:35	1	10	RAM 23	9
Week 17 vs SEA	4	5:55	1	10	SEA 13	13
NFCCG vs GB	2	0:54	1	10	GNB 19	1
SB vs KC	2	0:27	2	7	SFO 23	2
SB vs KC	3	2:40	1	1	KAN 1	1

With no kickout block like the previous version, the tight end has a little more to learn with his assignment. Additionally, the assignment is more difficult. A great blocking tight end like George Kittle is plenty capable of making this play go.

The first play side tight end will block it differently based on the front. The image below shows how the play looks when the end is head up or outside the tight end. If there is nobody in his interior gap, the tight end will step inside to seal a hole for the guard to pull through, and the play hits the C gap.

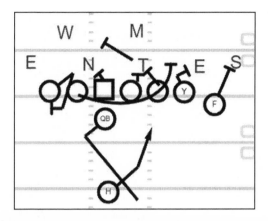

The image below shows the play hitting the D gap, when the tight end has to protect his inside gap.

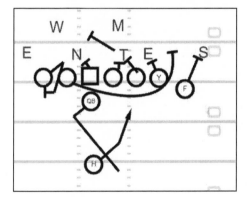

The fifth diagram shows the variation used for the week 17 touchdown.

This play was typically used late in games.

Why it Worked: The week 17 touchdown is clinic tape for digging out a 5 technique. . The left tackle does a nice job of showing to the 5 technique to allow the tight end to get inside position to seal open the C gap. With Bobby Wagner (the D gap player) getting outside of the tight end, a huge hole opens up.

Why it Didn't Work: The offensive line did not get much movement on a couple clips in week 6. The play gets chased down from behind with a player coming off the edge in week 8.

Counter – Down

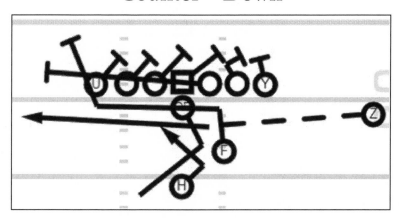

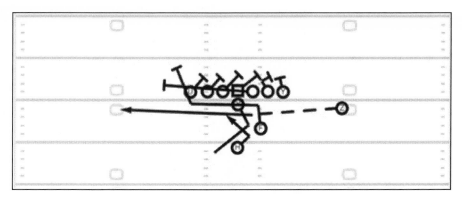

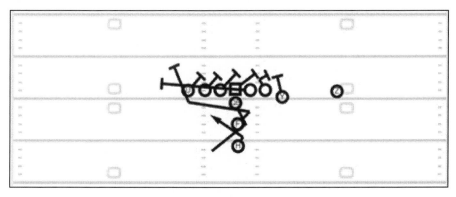

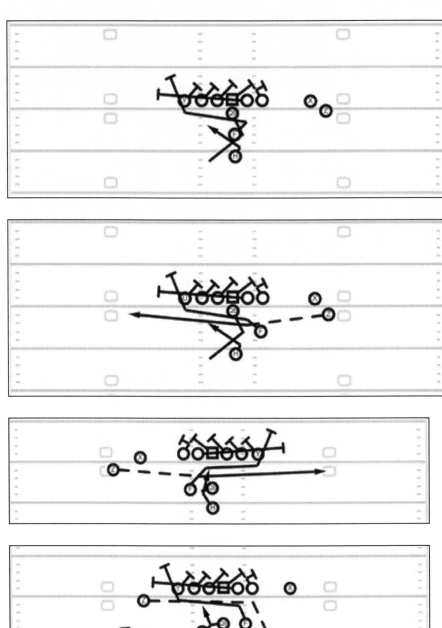

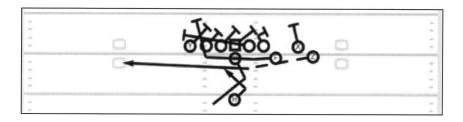

Average Yards per Play	4.3

1st Down		3rd/4th Down (includes RZ)	
Called	Average	Called	Success Rate
20	5.0	1	100%
2nd Down 6-1		**2nd Down 7+**	
Called	Average	Called	Average
9	3.4	2	3.0
Red Zone 10-0		**Red Zone 10-20**	
Called	Touchdown %	Called	Touchdown %
3	33%	3	0%

Bear		Over	
Called	Average	Called	Average
3	3.7	10	2.9
Under		**Mug**	
Called	Average	Called	Average
8	5.3	0	0.0
Wide		**Odd**	
Called	Average	Called	Average
0	0.0	10	5.5

Week	Quarter	Time	Down	ToGo	Location	Yards
Week 1 vs TB	3	5:43	1	10	SFO 25	10
Week 1 vs TB	3	5:11	1	10	SFO 35	13
Week 2 vs CIN	1	13:05	1	10	SFO 49	6
Week 3 vs PIT	1	15:00	1	10	SFO 25	5
Week 3 vs PIT	3	9:21	3	1	PIT 1	1
Week 3 vs PIT	3	5:42	1	10	SFO 25	9
Week 3 vs PIT	4	9:21	2	5	PIT 38	19
Week 3 vs PIT	4	8:53	1	10	PIT 19	6
Week 3 vs PIT	4	3:37	1	10	PIT 13	3
Week 3 vs PIT	4	2:00	1	9	PIT 9	4
Week 5 vs CLE	1	10:23	1	10	SFO 26	6
Week 5 vs CLE	3	6:39	2	4	SFO 38	-2
Week 5 vs CLE	4	3:38	1	10	SFO 20	3
Week 6 vs LA	3	7:22	1	10	RAM 24	1
Week 6 vs LA	3	5:55	1	2	RAM 2	0
Week 7 vs WAS	1	4:44	2	9	SFO 40	2
Week 7 vs WAS	3	13:56	1	10	WAS 42	5
Week 7 vs WAS	3	13:28	2	5	WAS 37	1
Week 8 vs CAR	2	3:48	1	10	SFO 37	4
Week 10 vs SEA	1	3:40	1	10	SEA 12	3
Week 10 vs SEA	2	8:00	2	3	SFO 44	0
Week 10 vs SEA	2	1:04	1	10	SFO 2	3
Week 16 vs LAR	4	14:47	1	10	SFO 6	5
DIV vs MIN	2	9:05	2	3	MIN 23	4
DIV vs MIN	3	2:49	2	4	SFO 23	3
DIV vs MIN	4	11:55	2	8	SFO 16	4
NFCCG vs GB	1	14:23	2	5	SFO 30	4
NFCCG vs GB	1	7:29	1	10	GNB 38	6
NFCCG vs GB	2	4:20	2	3	GNB 28	1
NFCCG vs GB	4	14:34	1	10	GNB 48	4
SB vs KC	1	11:09	2	3	KAN 33	1
SB vs KC	2	0:59	1	10	SFO 20	3

The counter scheme was a nice play for the 49ers in 2019. Defenses like to load the line of scrimmage with a bear front or with the sam and will walked up to stop outside zone. Counter gives the offense a nice way to wash down the loaded line of scrimmage and get downhill quickly.

Most coaches prefer to run power and counter to the 3 technique side. This allows for a double team at the point of attack with the play side guard and tackle. This can still be achieved against teams that play an "under" front, by motioning/shifting the tight end or using a second tight end. The first diagram shows a 22 personnel variation with fake jet motion to the side they are running the counter to. This variation ensures that they get the 3 technique play side vs "under" fronts. Good examples of this can be seen with back to back clips starting at 3Q 5:23 in Week 1.

The image below shows the play against an over front.

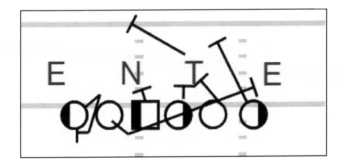

Counter – Strong – Down was a popular call against odd fronts. In Week 3 vs PIT with the Steelers using odd fronts most of the game, the scheme allowed tight end George Kittle to get in on the double team action with the play side tackle. The image below shows the combination vs a 3-4 front.

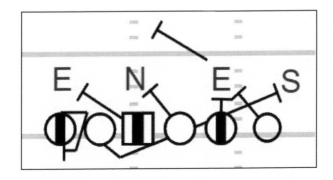

The 7th diagram shows the version used in week 7 on 1st and 10.

The pistol variation can be seen in week 10 1Q.

Why it Worked: All of the week 3 clips area great teaching tape for how to run the counter scheme against an odd front. Sound execution for each block. This scheme averaged 6.7 yards per carry in this game.

Why it Didn't Work: In week 5, the pulling guard did not get his head up quickly to pick up the 5 technique getting upfield quickly.

Counter – Arc

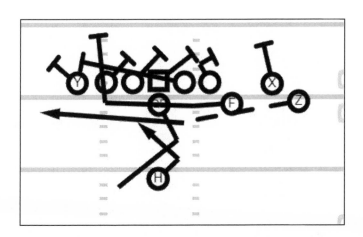

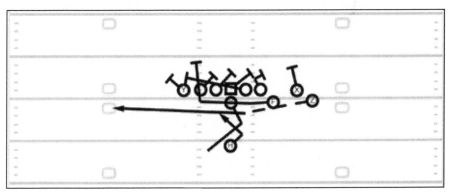

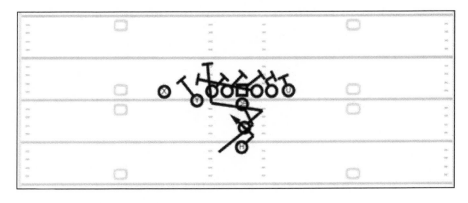

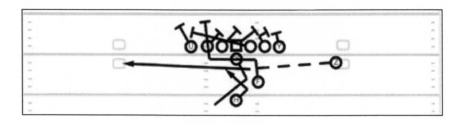

Average Yards per Play	3.2

1st Down		3rd/4th Down (includes RZ)	
Called	Average	Called	Success Rate
8	3.6	0	0%
2nd Down 6-1		**2nd Down 7+**	
Called	Average	Called	Average
1	0.0	3	3.0
Red Zone 10-0		**Red Zone 10-20**	
Called	Touchdown %	Called	Touchdown %
1	100%	0	0%

Bear		Over	
Called	Average	Called	Average
3	-0.3	3	3.0
Under		**Mug**	
Called	Average	Called	Average
5	4.6	0	0.0
Wide		**Odd**	
Called	Average	Called	Average
0	0.0	0	0.0

Week	Quarter	Time	Down	ToGo	Location	Yards
Week 2 vs CIN	2	10:11	1	2	CIN 2	2
Week 2 vs CIN	3	6:09	1	10	CIN 28	-4
Week 5 vs CLE	1	12:57	2	10	CLE 41	1
Week 5 vs CLE	2	9:56	2	7	SFO 43	4
Week 8 vs CAR	4	3:29	2	8	CAR 39	4
Week 10 vs SEA	1	15:00	1	10	SFO 25	1
Week 10 vs SEA	4	7:41	1	10	SEA 23	7
Week 10 vs SEA	OT	4:48	1	10	SEA 38	8
Week 10 vs SEA	OT	4:10	2	2	SEA 30	0
Week 16 vs LAR	4	13:27	1	10	SFO 18	3
DIV vs MIN	4	8:59	1	10	SFO 21	8
DIV vs MIN	4	7:25	1	10	SFO 40	4

One subtle variation the 49ers used is the "arc" tag for the front side defensive end. This tag has a few key schematic advantages.

There is an important coaching point for the arc block. The play side TE takes a jab-step down first. This freezes the defensive end and makes the kick out block for the back side guard easier.

This technique was typically used against defenses that liked to play the tight end with head up leverage or inside shade. This arcing prevents the tight end (and play side tackle) to have to down block 1 on 1.

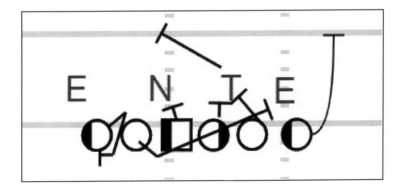

Fake jet motion really messed with play side line backers with counter action. Often times the tight end would block the first linebacker, leaving the backside linebacker for the fullback. This also has the added benefit of the tackle/guard double team to not have to leave for the back side linebacker.

Why it Worked: In 4Q and OT 4:48 week 10, the front side 6i gets upfield quickly and creates a nice lane for the running back to get down hill fast.

Why it Didn't Work: In the first play of week 10 and 3Q week 2, the center is not able to get his base block against a bear nose.

Counter Weak - No TE Play Side

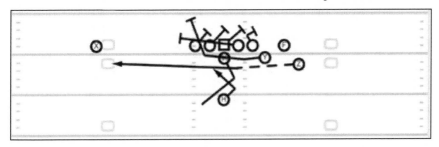

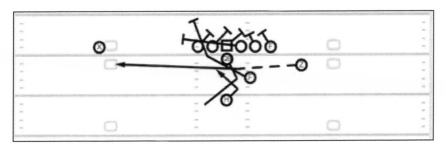

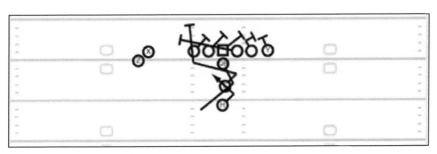

Bear		Over	
Called	Average	Called	Average
2	2.5	3	7.3
Under		Mug	
Called	Average	Called	Average
3	3.7	0	0.0
Wide		Odd	
Called	Average	Called	Average
0	0.0	0	0.0

Average Yards per Play	4.8

1st Down		3rd/4th Down (includes RZ)	
Called	Average	Called	Success Rate
5	2.8	0	0%
2nd Down 6-1		**2nd Down 7+**	
Called	Average	Called	Average
1	2.0	2	11.0
Red Zone 10-0		**Red Zone 10-20**	
Called	Touchdown %	Called	Touchdown %
0	0%	0	0%

Week	Quarter	Time	Down	ToGo	Location	Yards
Week 2 vs CIN	1	3:24	1	10	CIN 45	6
Week 2 vs CIN	2	1:05	2	10	SFO 44	16
Week 5 vs CLE	3	5:12	1	10	SFO 46	0
Week 6 vs LA	1	5:07	1	10	RAM 25	4
Week 6 vs LA	3	1:35	2	8	RAM 45	6
Week 9 vs ARI	1	2:58	1	5	CRD 43	1
Week 12 vs GB	4	8:42	2	6	SFO 48	2
Week 14 vs NO	3	12:36	1	10	SFO 25	3

Running counter to the weak side is a complimentary play and tendency breaker for the 49ers.

One adjustment to the scheme against over fronts is to lock the front side tackle on the 5 technique. This adjustment keeps the tackle from having to block a linebacker in space, and gives the offense two pullers through the open B Gap. The image below shows the adjustment.

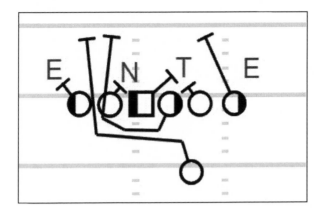

Why it Worked: Against the Rams under front, running counter to the weak side allows for the play side double team. They 49ers get a nice gain in week 6 against that under front.

Why it Didn't Work: In week 14, the Saints ran a balanced bear front. The weak side linebacker was able to scrape over the top untouched as the play side 3 tech takes the double team to the ground. In week 5 the Browns had an extra support player on the weak side of the formation.

Duo

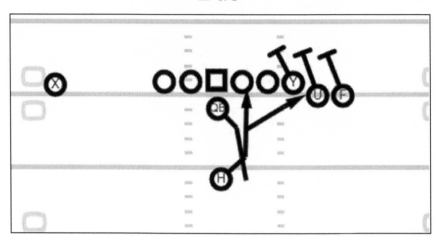

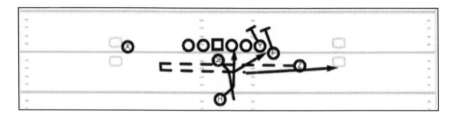

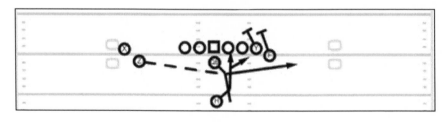

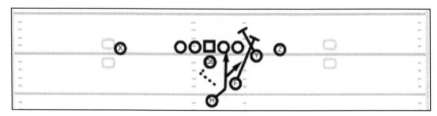

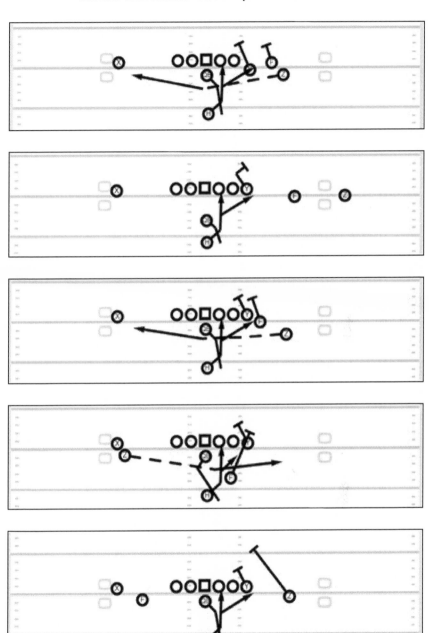

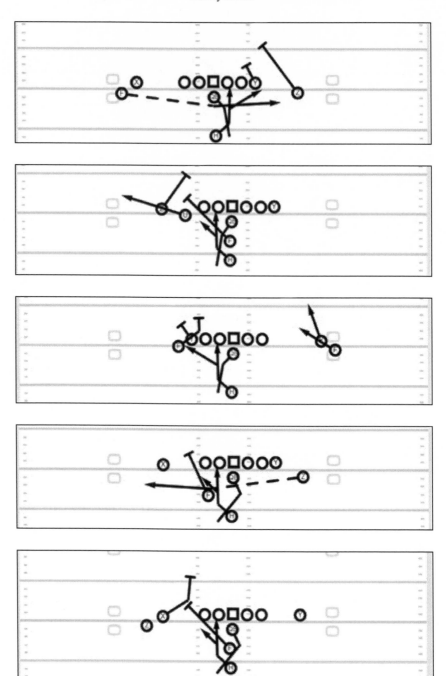

Average Yards per Play	3.1

1st Down		3rd/4th Down (includes RZ)	
Called	Average	Called	Success Rate
9	4.3	9	38%
2nd Down 6-1		2nd Down 7+	
Called	Average	Called	Average
9	2.1	5	3.4
Red Zone 10-0		Red Zone 10-20	
Called	Touchdown %	Called	Touchdown %
7	29%	3	0%

Bear		Over	
Called	Average	Called	Average
6	2.5	7	3.0
Under		Mug	
Called	Average	Called	Average
8	4.4	1	0.0
Wide		Odd	
Called	Average	Called	Average
0	0.0	3	1.3

Week	Quarter	Time	Down	ToGo	Location	Yards
Week 1 vs TB	1	7:32	1	10	SFO 9	12
Week 1 vs TB	2	4:34	1	10	TAM 15	3
Week 1 vs TB	4	11:44	3	1	SFO 11	1
Week 1 vs TB	4	10:10	2	15	SFO 7	1
Week 3 vs PIT	3	10:43	1	3	PIT 3	0
Week 3 vs PIT	4	4:49	2	1	PIT 15	0
Week 6 vs LA	1	8:39	2	1	SFO 34	2
Week 6 vs LA	1	3:44	1	2	RAM 2	2
Week 6 vs LA	2	13:23	2	7	RAM 7	6
Week 6 vs LA	2	2:32	2	9	SFO 2	3
Week 6 vs LA	3	13:27	2	1	RAM 1	0
Week 6 vs LA	3	9:55	3	1	RAM 48	9
Week 6 vs LA	3	0:09	1	10	RAM 35	9
Week 6 vs LA	4	12:54	3	1	RAM 15	0
Week 7 vs WAS	2	3:18	2	1	SFO 38	4
Week 7 vs WAS	4	15:00	1	10	WAS 44	7
Week 7 vs WAS	4	14:18	2	3	WAS 37	2
Week 7 vs WAS	4	13:18	3	1	WAS 35	0
Week 7 vs WAS	4	3:42	2	1	WAS 36	6
Week 8 vs CAR	3	10:45	2	1	SFO 34	3
Week 11 vs ARI	4	0:21	2	8	CRD 28	4
Week 12 vs GB	1	13:07	1	2	GNB 2	2
Week 12 vs GB	1	6:32	2	8	GNB 49	3
Week 12 vs GB	2	9:51	3	30	SFO 8	5
Week 14 vs NO	1	9:14	1	5	NOR 5	0
Week 15 vs ATL	1	7:44	3	1	SFO 21	7
Week 15 vs ATL	4	13:44	1	10	SFO 13	4
Week 16 vs LAR	1	10:08	2	1	RAM 9	2
Week 16 vs LAR	2	14:18	2	1	SFO 34	0
DIV vs MIN	4	1:54	3	2	SFO 48	1
DIV vs MIN	4	1:49	4	1	SFO 49	1
NFCCG vs GB	1	14:00	3	1	SFO 34	0

The 49ers will run Duo out of any 11/20/12/21/22/13/23 personnel set (basically everything but 10 personnel). In most NFL offenses, this play is typically reserved for short yardage situations. The 49ers used it for these situations, but also mixed it in with their middle of the field offense (regular 1st and 2nd downs). This is most likely the case due to the heavy boxes that the 49ers often see.

Teams like in in short yardage situations because it is a down hill run, even more so than inside zone. It is taught like power, but without the puller. The offensive line will aggressively double team the down lineman up to the linebackers.

The play is drawn below vs an under front. With no pulling guard, Duo allows the offense to seal off a 3 technique in a bear or under front on the back side of the play. In short yardage situations, back blocks on 3 techniques are hard blocks for centers. I saw this a few times when the Rams ran Power on third and shorts in my 2017 study of their offense. Additionally, without having to back block, the center can help double team on the play side 1 technique.

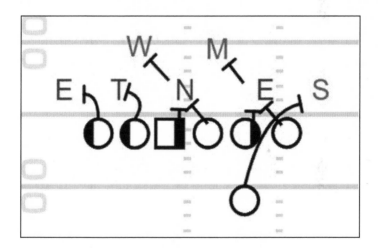

One particular benefit of Duo is the ability to bounce the play off the front side, and get the RB in the open field vs a corner. This run scheme can be often featured if a defense is missing a starting corner, or if the corner to the front side is a poor tackler. A good example of this can be seen at 15:00 4Q week 7.

Duo was a big part of the 49ers game plan in week 6 and week 7. Week 6 featured many short yardage situations, as well as a late lead that the 49ers were sitting on. With the sloppy weather in week 7, the downhill run scheme gave the 49ers a safe way to move the ball.

The week 11 clip shows a tremendous cut from Coleman to pop out the backside of the offensive line. This variation is the one with the TE releasing to the flat, shown in the 11th diagram.

The 12th diagram shows an "insert" variation with a shield slant RPO attached. This play can be found in week 14. The 13th diagram shows a typical way the 49ers would run this away from the tight end. Two clips of this can be seen in week 16. In week 6 2Q 13:23, Garoppolo threw a "now" screen to the single receiver on the back side of the 3 TE variation (1st diagram).

Why it Worked: In the week 6 3rd &1 conversion, the 49ers get an awesome double team from the C and PSG to clear a huge hole. The week 15 conversion (14th diagram) shows a well-designed version that is run without a TE vs a bear front. The PS 3-tech gets double teamed by the PSG and PST and the OLB gets kicked out by the FB. The slot WR does a nice job of occupying the rolled down safety as well. In week 12, Coleman ran behind Kittle and Juszczyk

Why it Didn't Work: In week 6 4Q 12:54, Kittle is unable to get the front side down block on a 5 tech. The Rams had loaded the box here as well. This is also the case in week 7 4Q 13:18. An errant throw on the RPO variation in week 14 caused an incompletion.

Crack Toss

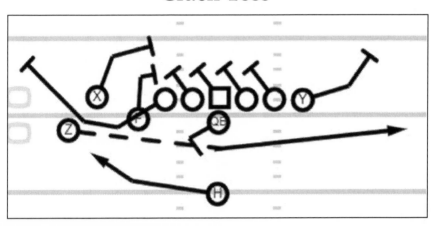

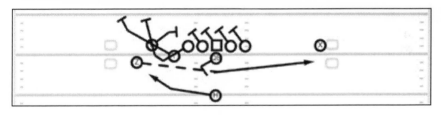

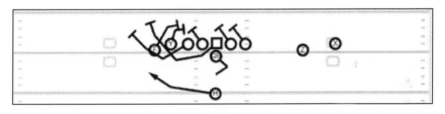

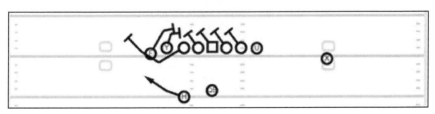

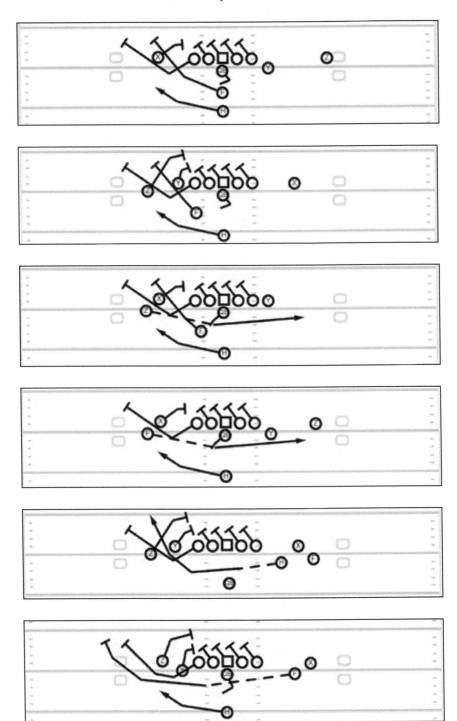

Average Yards per Play	4.0

1st Down		3rd/4th Down (includes RZ)	
Called	Average	Called	Success Rate
17	3.5	1	100%
2nd Down 6-1		**2nd Down 7+**	
Called	Average	Called	Average
2	5.5	4	5.8
Red Zone 10-0		**Red Zone 10-20**	
Called	Touchdown %	Called	Touchdown %
1	0%	0	0%

Week	Quarter	Time	Down	ToGo	Location	Yards
Week 1 vs TB	2	11:51	1	10	SFO 8	0
Week 1 vs TB	2	2:49	1	10	TAM 29	5
Week 1 vs TB	4	2:30	2	10	TAM 31	2
Week 2 vs CIN	4	12:53	2	7	SFO 43	11
Week 3 vs PIT	1	9:04	1	10	SFO 49	-18
Week 5 vs CLE	2	10:34	1	10	SFO 40	3
Week 5 vs CLE	3	7:47	1	10	SFO 17	15
Week 6 vs LA	1	14:55	1	10	SFO 17	1
Week 6 vs LA	1	6:11	1	10	RAM 47	5
Week 6 vs LA	2	14:05	1	6	RAM 6	-1
Week 8 vs CAR	2	13:46	1	10	CAR 27	17
Week 8 vs CAR	2	8:47	2	12	SFO 43	1
Week 9 vs ARI	2	2:46	1	10	CRD 33	19
Week 9 vs ARI	3	8:31	1	10	SFO 48	2
Week 9 vs ARI	3	7:13	1	10	CRD 24	-2
Week 9 vs ARI	4	2:27	3	3	SFO 48	3
Week 13 vs BAL	1	5:35	1	10	SFO 30	6
Week 14 vs NO	4	3:31	2	6	NOR 30	6
Week 15 vs ATL	1	1:06	1	10	ATL 25	1
Week 15 vs ATL	2	7:01	1	10	SFO 25	5
Week 15 vs ATL	3	2:07	1	10	SFO 48	-2
NFCCG vs GB	3	8:03	2	3	SFO 28	5
SB vs KC	2	8:42	2	9	SFO 21	9
SB vs KC	3	13:14	1	10	SFO 50	4

Bear		Over	
Called	Average	Called	Average
6	3.3	13	6.6
Under		Mug	
Called	Average	Called	Average
3	3.3	1	-1.0
Wide		Odd	
Called	Average	Called	Average
0	0.0	1	-18.0

When defenses like to get into bear fronts and "tilt" 4-3 looks to stop the outside zone scheme, crack toss is a great way to get the ball out on the edge away from the mess inside. The image below shows the play drawn up against a bear front.

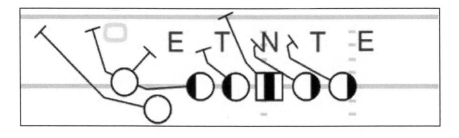

Crack toss is a great concept against man coverage. The receivers/tight ends that crack can get a "2 for 1" block and create a softer surface for the pullers and running back.

The receivers/fullbacks/tight ends outside of the play side tackle will crack down on the EMOL (end man on the line of scrimmage) and the first second level defender. The important coaching point for these blocks is to not let anybody cross their face. The first puller will block the support player. If there is a second puller, he will lead up the hole for the running back.

When Shanahan was the OC for the Falcons' Superbowl against the Patriots, he featured crack toss in his game plan. The Patriots typically play more man coverage, and are often lining up in their bear/"diamond" front. Crack toss is a great answer against both.

The fourth diagram shows a variation the 49ers used out of shotgun in week 5. A shotgun variation of the third diagram was used in week 6

The fifth diagram shows a I formation - weak side variation used in week 5 3Q that went for a nice gain.

The 10th diagram shows a variation used in the Super Bowl where the fake jet motion leads with the pulling tackle. A creative way to get a +1 blocker at the point of attack.

The 4Q week 1 clip shows a funny play where both Kittle and Staley whiff on their pull blocks at the exact same time.

Why it Worked: A common theme for this play working is a strong crack block(s). Week 5 shows a good clip of Deebo Samuel sealing off the defensive end with great technique. This block doesn't have to be the old school kill shot, but the defender can not work over the top

Why it Didn't Work: The key block(s) is the crack block from the WR/TE's. If they allow the defender to get over the top of them, the play is often strung out to the sideline. The image below shows the defensive end working over the top to string the play out, and force the ball back inside to the pursuit. The first clip from week 1 shows an example of this.

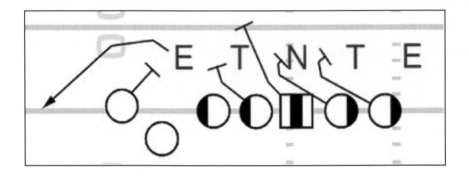

Trap

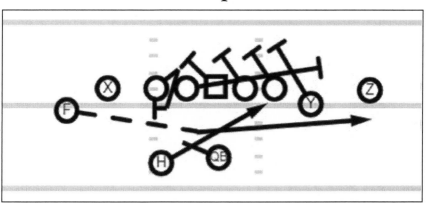

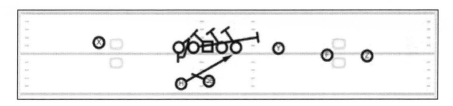

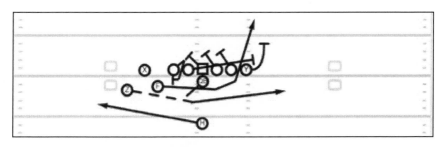

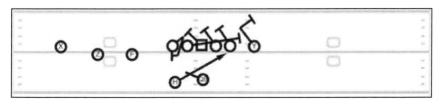

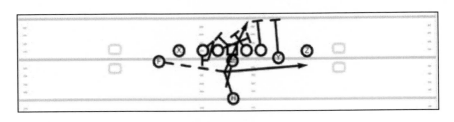

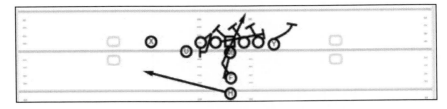

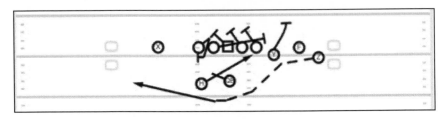

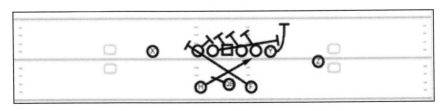

Average Yards per Play	7.8

1st Down		3rd/4th Down (includes RZ)	
Called	Average	Called	Success Rate
11	12.2	13	23%
2nd Down 6-1		2nd Down 7+	
Called	Average	Called	Average
4	4.5	6	4.5
Red Zone 10-0		Red Zone 10-20	
Called	Touchdown %	Called	Touchdown %
2	100%	4	25%

The 2019 San Francisco 49ers Complete Offensive Manual

Week	Quarter	Time	Down	ToGo	Location	Yards
Week 5 vs CLE	2	2:48	3	5	CLE 31	4
Week 5 vs CLE	4	8:04	3	27	SFO 9	7
Week 7 vs WAS	2	0:07	3	15	SFO 46	2
Week 8 vs CAR	2	9:18	1	10	SFO 45	3
Week 8 vs CAR	2	2:00	1	5	CAR 48	48
Week 8 vs CAR	3	7:20	1	10	CAR 20	20
Week 8 vs CAR	4	10:35	3	9	SFO 48	1
Week 9 vs ARI	1	2:17	3	4	CRD 42	5
Week 9 vs ARI	1	1:34	1	10	CRD 37	0
Week 9 vs ARI	3	13:16	2	10	SFO 41	1
Week 11 vs ARI	2	0:16	3	18	CRD 24	-1
Week 12 vs GB	1	5:32	1	10	GNB 41	25
Week 12 vs GB	2	1:56	1	10	SFO 39	15
Week 12 vs GB	2	1:39	1	10	GNB 46	4
Week 14 vs NO	2	1:46	2	6	NOR 28	5
Week 14 vs NO	2	0:45	1	10	NOR 10	10
Week 14 vs NO	4	10:34	1	10	NOR 16	2
Week 15 vs ATL	1	5:07	2	2	ATL 47	2
Week 15 vs ATL	1	3:42	3	3	ATL 38	2
Week 15 vs ATL	2	14:18	2	10	ATL 13	6
Week 16 vs LAR	3	9:19	2	10	SFO 44	5
Week 16 vs LAR	3	3:38	3	17	SFO 18	13
Week 16 vs LAR	4	1:17	1	10	SFO 37	1
Week 17 vs SEA	2	0:42	2	10	SFO 31	2
Week 17 vs SEA	4	7:58	1	10	SEA 39	6
DIV vs MIN	1	3:29	2	7	SFO 38	10
DIV vs MIN	2	12:39	2	10	SFO 47	3
DIV vs MIN	3	11:36	2	4	MIN 19	2
DIV vs MIN	4	5:51	3	6	SFO 44	5
NFCCG vs GB	1	6:01	3	8	GNB 36	36
NFCCG vs GB	2	9:17	2	6	GNB 9	9
NFCCG vs GB	2	3:34	3	2	GNB 27	10
NFCCG vs GB	4	13:05	3	3	GNB 41	2
NFCCG vs GB	4	4:22	3	2	GNB 23	-1

Bear		Over	
Called	Average	Called	Average
7	8.4	15	8.7
Under		Mug	
Called	Average	Called	Average
3	2.7	2	4.5
Wide		Odd	
Called	Average	Called	Average
4	7.8	2	13.5

Trap was an explosive play for the 49ers in 2019. A few long runs came off this concept. This play was also a 3rd and long play call, when the defensive line is getting upfield quickly.

The 49ers have a few different ways they will run this. Most of the time, the will trap the EMOL (end man on the line of scrimmage. When run to the tight end, the tight end has similar rules for what he does on Counter. Head up/Inside leverage = arc release.

Occasionally, they will trap a 3 technique. A good clip of this can be seen week 8 2Q 9:18 and week 9 3Q.

The second diagram shows the version used for the 48 yard touchdown in week 8.

The third diagram shows the 20 yard TD in week 8. This scheme is a nice way to get misdirection with your trap scheme.

The 6th diagram shows a fullback trap used against a bear front in week 15 1Q 5:07.

The 8th diagram shows a variation with a slice block to help seal the backside of the play, and allow the backside tackle to take the 3 technique without having to squeeze hinge back for the EMOL.

Why it Worked: The Panthers got caught in a blitz on the long TD in week 8. With the blitz coming off the weak edge, the force player gets way to far upfield, and the backside tackle washes down the DE trying to get to the B gap. With the nose working to the front side A gap and the back side LB scraping hard, a huge hole opened up on the back side. The play is diagrammed below.

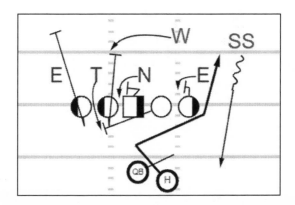

Trap was a great play call for the 49ers in the NFCCG. The play hit for their first touchdown against a bear/diamond front. The guard trapped the 3 technique, and the unblocked edge player rushed upfield to get after the quarterback in a third and long situation.

Why it Didn't Work: In the 3rd down play in week 5, the 3 tech was able to spin out of the double team, and the backer scraped well over the top. In the week 15 3rd down, the offensive line does a nice job, but the running back decides to cut it back when he didn't need to.

Pin/Pull

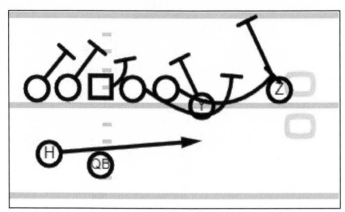

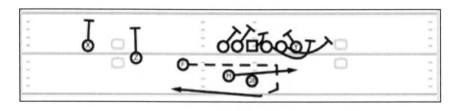

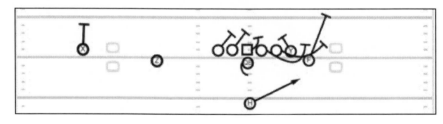

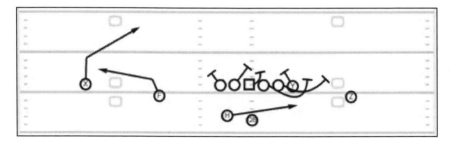

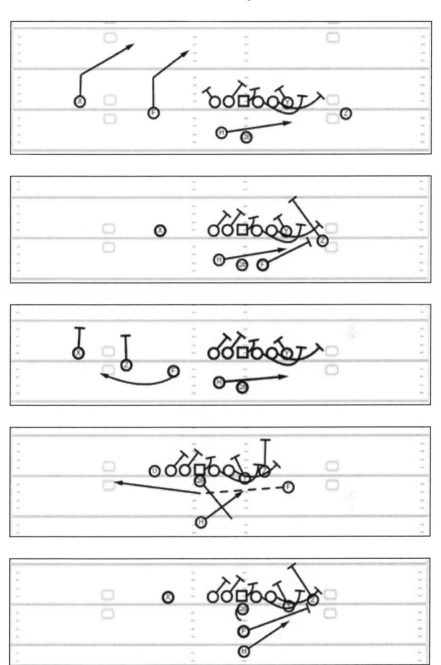

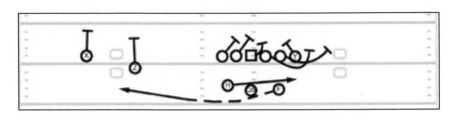

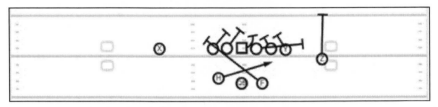

Average Yards per Play	5.5

1st Down		3rd/4th Down (includes RZ)	
Called	Average	Called	Success Rate
14	6.9	0	0%
2nd Down 6-1		**2nd Down 7+**	
Called	Average	Called	Average
3	0.7	2	3.0
Red Zone 10-0		**Red Zone 10-20**	
Called	Touchdown %	Called	Touchdown %
0	0%	6	33%

Bear		Over	
Called	Average	Called	Average
2	6.0	8	8.3
Under		**Mug**	
Called	Average	Called	Average
4	2.3	0	0.0
Wide		**Odd**	
Called	Average	Called	Average
0	0.0	5	3.6

Week	Quarter	Time	Down	ToGo	Location	Yards
Week 3 vs PIT	1	11:11	2	6	SFO 29	8
Week 3 vs PIT	4	10:22	1	10	SFO 25	7
Week 5 vs CLE	2	2:00	1	10	CLE 19	19
Week 7 vs WAS	1	5:21	1	10	SFO 39	1
Week 7 vs WAS	2	12:22	1	10	WAS 19	-2
Week 7 vs WAS	3	7:03	2	9	WAS 14	4
Week 10 vs SEA	3	4:14	2	10	SFO 40	2
Week 10 vs SEA	4	15:00	1	10	SFO 36	0
Week 10 vs SEA	4	10:22	1	10	SFO 31	4
Week 10 vs SEA	4	7:09	2	3	SEA 16	-5
Week 12 vs GB	3	14:31	1	22	SFO 13	6
Week 13 vs BAL	2	1:13	1	20	SFO 34	8
Week 13 vs BAL	3	12:03	1	10	SFO 20	4
Week 15 vs ATL	2	1:21	1	10	ATL 23	16
Week 16 vs LAR	2	12:14	1	10	RAM 19	19
Week 17 vs SEA	1	1:11	1	10	SEA 36	6
Week 17 vs SEA	2	6:58	1	10	SEA 15	0
Week 17 vs SEA	4	7:17	2	4	SEA 33	-1
NFCCG vs GB	2	11:49	1	10	GNB 24	9

Pin/Pull was a common call against the odd fronts of Pittsburg and Washington. The image below shows how the play is blocked up against these fronts.

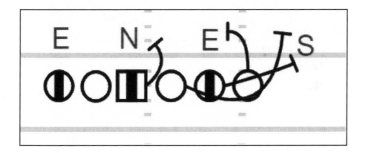

The blocking looks identical in an under front with the nose shading the center. When the nose is in a 2i, the guard will down block him, and the center will pull. This version was used in week 10 and is shown below.

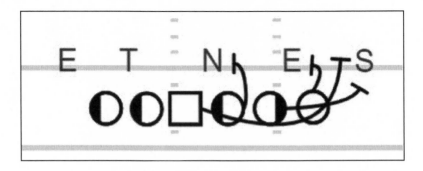

When the defense plays an over front, the tackle will down block on the 3 technique. A few of these clips can be seen in week 10. With these versions, the backside tackle will typically lock the 5 technique and the QB will RPO the backside inside linebacker. This version is shown below.

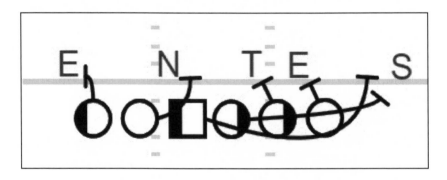

Against bear fronts, and teams that like to choke the tight end, a Wing T "Down" version was used, with just the guard pulling to kick out. The 11th diagram shows this version with a slice block from the fullback to get the backside end. The front side blocking adjustment is drawn up below.

Why it Worked: The Wing T "Down" versions were very good for the 49ers against loaded fronts. The TD in week 16 was off this action.

The touchdown run in week 5 was against an over front with the sam walked up. The 49ers called it with a backside lock tag and a dragon route combination as the RPO. This clip is teach tape for how to block the concept.

In week 15, Garoppolo hits Kittle on the double slant RPO against outside divider leverage on the slot receiver.

Why it Didn't Work: In over fronts, the end can line up in a 6 technique. This block can be tricky for tight ends. Clowney made a few plays in week 10 from this alignment.

Clowney also sacked Garoppolo coming off the backside edge in week 10. Garoppolo pulled for the RPO read, and Clowney beat the tackle to get in the backfield right away.

In week 10, one of the receivers drops a slant pass on the RPO aspect.

Zone Rollback

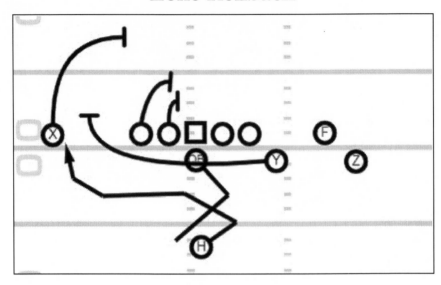

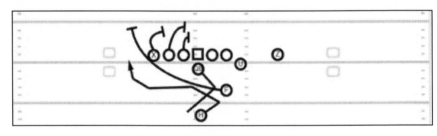

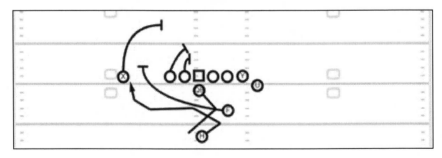

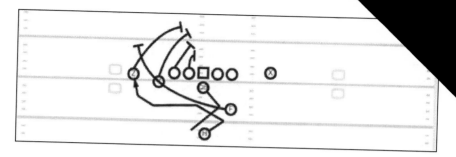

Average Yards per Play	6.9

1st Down		3rd/4th Down (includes RZ)	
Called	Average	Called	Success Rate
8	6.4	0	0%
2nd Down 6-1		2nd Down 7+	
Called	Average	Called	Average
1	13.0	1	5.0
Red Zone 10-0		Red Zone 10-20	
Called	Touchdown %	Called	Touchdown %
0	0%	0	0%

Bear		Over	
Called	Average	Called	Average
1	9.0	7	7.9
Under		Mug	
Called	Average	Called	Average
1	0.0	0	0.0
Wide		Odd	
Called	Average	Called	Average
0	0.0	1	5.0

Bobby Peters

		Time	Down	ToGo	Location	Yards
		4:00	1	10	SFO 43	12
		14:00	1	14	CIN 40	15
		13:30	1	10	CIN 25	9
		7:59	2	10	SFO 25	5
		12:40	1	10	CLE 49	12
		9:35	1	10	RAV 48	5
		7:34	1	10	ATL 34	-6
		13:49	1	10	SFO 21	4
Week 17 vs SEA	1	4:56	1	10	SFO 6	0
Week 17 vs SEA	4	9:21	2	3	SFO 32	13

Zone rollback is one of the 49ers constraint plays for their zone scheme. The misdirection takes advantage of defensive ends that are taught to squeeze a tackles down block hard. The end is typically left unblocked, "bluffed", by the fullback or tight end wrapping around.

Zone rollback is great when defensive ends want to wrong arm the slice block. The slicer will bluff him and pull around for the send level support. The diagram below shows this action. The play is drawn up against an over front. The 49ers saw this front most often when running this scheme.

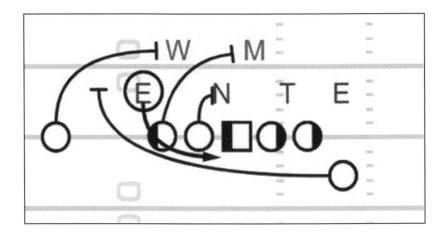

When run to the tight end, the 5 technique is still left unblocked. The tight end will climb to the next level.

A key detail for the offensive line is to not double team like they would on zone runs. The focus needs to be getting up to the second level and seal off linebackers.

A key coaching point is for the offensive line to aim for the defender's back. This will prevent them from angling the play over the top, and force them to chase from behind

Why it Worked: The 1st and 14 clip from week 2 is teaching tape for this concept. Text book execution.

In the week 17 clip, Juszczyk end up blocking the defensive end because he fights hard to stay upfield. The running back cuts under that block to pick up a nice gain.

Why it Didn't Work: In week 15, the 3 technique on the front side of the zone action cuts inside into the A gap and blows up the play in the backfield.

Jet Sweeps

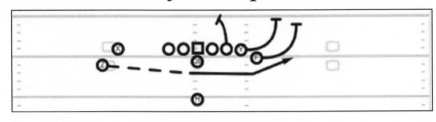

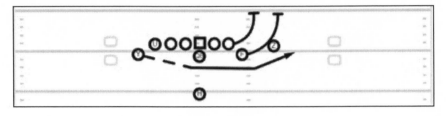

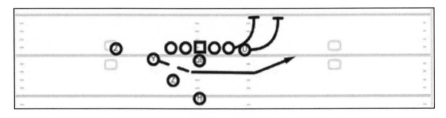

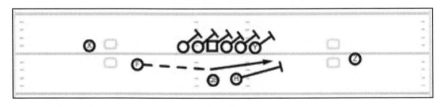

Average Yards per Play	4.4

1st Down		3rd/4th Down (includes RZ)	
Called	Average	Called	Success Rate
9	4.8	1	0%
2nd Down 6-1		**2nd Down 7+**	
Called	Average	Called	Average
2	10.0	4	2.3
Red Zone 10-0		**Red Zone 10-20**	
Called	Touchdown %	Called	Touchdown %
1	0%	4	0%

Bear		Over	
Called	Average	Called	Average
2	1.5	7	4.1
Under		**Mug**	
Called	Average	Called	Average
5	7.0	1	1.0
Wide		**Odd**	
Called	Average	Called	Average
0	0.0	0	0.0

Week	Quarter	Time	Down	ToGo	Location	Yards
Week 1 vs TB	2	9:12	2	9	SFO 21	1
Week 2 vs CIN	1	12:31	2	4	CIN 45	2
Week 5 vs CLE	1	9:50	2	4	SFO 32	18
Week 5 vs CLE	1	3:34	1	10	CLE 29	3
Week 7 vs WAS	1	1:36	2	9	SFO 47	2
Week 7 vs WAS	4	9:48	3	2	WAS 2	-2
Week 8 vs CAR	1	11:10	1	10	CAR 19	2
Week 10 vs SEA	1	2:42	2	12	SEA 14	4
Week 10 vs SEA	3	11:37	1	10	SEA 41	4
Week 12 vs GB	2	4:13	1	10	GNB 17	0
Week 13 vs BAL	3	5:14	1	10	RAV 16	-3
Week 14 vs NO	1	4:00	2	14	SFO 21	2
Week 15 vs ATL	2	7:01	1	10	SFO 25	5
Week 16 vs LAR	2	14:55	1	10	SFO 25	9
Week 17 vs SEA	4	9:55	1	10	SFO 25	7
SB vs KC	2	8:09	1	10	SFO 30	16

Jet sweeps are an auxiliary run in the 49ers system. The occasional use of this play is enough to keep the defense honest and respect the fake jet sweep action. With the 49ers tying the fake jet sweep action with basically every run scheme, this is an important element in the overall success of the 49ers run game.

This section also includes jet action outside zone schemes. These versions are bolded. They are also included in their respective outside zone section.

The 49ers often used George Kittle on jet sweeps. This is a great use of personnel because he is great with the ball in space, and is incredibly powerful and fast in the open field.

With a single tight end on the side of the jet action, the tight end and tackle will arc release and leave the 5 technique unblocked.

With a 2 tight end surface, both tight ends would arc release. They would leave the 6 technique unblocked.

Why it Worked: In week 5, the tight end and tackle arc the 5 tech and get up on the force player and inside linebacker with nice blocks.

Why it Didn't Work: The sloppy conditions made cutting hard for the ball carrier in week 7 and week 13.

Reverses/End Arounds

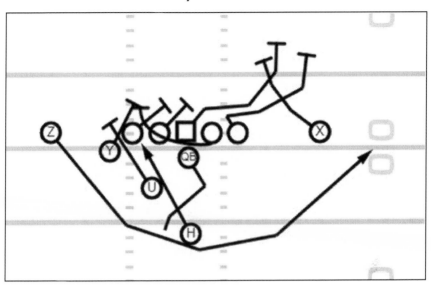

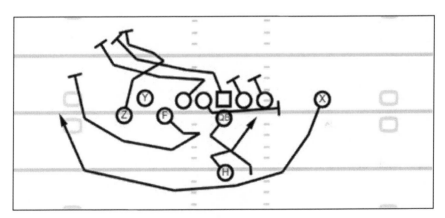

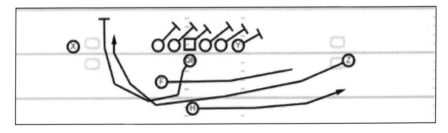

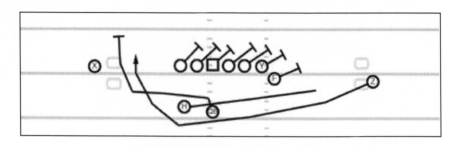

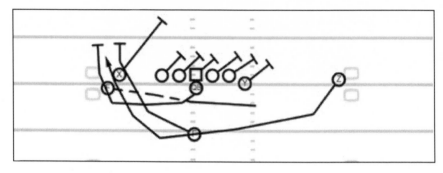

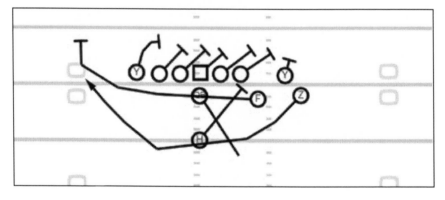

Average Yards per Play	17.3

1st Down		3rd/4th Down (includes RZ)	
Called	Average	Called	Success Rate
6	15.3	0	0%
2nd Down 6-1		**2nd Down 7+**	
Called	Average	Called	Average
1	30.0	5	17.2
Red Zone 10-0		**Red Zone 10-20**	
Called	Touchdown %	Called	Touchdown %
0	0%	0	0%

Bear		Over	
Called	Average	Called	Average
3	24.3	4	9.5
Under		**Mug**	
Called	Average	Called	Average
4	23.0	0	0.0
Wide		**Odd**	
Called	Average	Called	Average
0	0.0	1	5.0

Week	Quarter	Time	Down	ToGo	Location	Yards
Week 2 vs CIN	4	3:17	2	7	SFO 29	5
Week 5 vs CLE	1	7:57	2	7	CLE 24	15
Week 8 vs CAR	3	11:15	1	10	SFO 25	9
Week 13 vs BAL	2	11:58	1	10	SFO 25	20
Week 14 vs NO	4	4:22	2	10	SFO 35	31
Week 17 vs SEA	1	0:32	2	4	SEA 30	30
Week 17 vs SEA	4	2:52	2	7	SFO 24	3
DIV vs MIN	2	10:49	1	10	MIN 41	6
NFCCG vs GB	3	7:18	1	10	SFO 33	11
NFCCG vs GB	3	6:07	2	8	SFO 46	32
SB vs KC	1	12:33	1	10	SFO 28	32
SB vs KC	3	13:37	1	10	SFO 36	14

Reverses and end arounds were the source of some

explosive plays for the 49ers. They called two reverses in the Super Bowl for nice gains.

Deebo Samuel runs like a running back, so getting his speed coming around on the reverse was a critical part of the success of the play. He has a great feel for this action.

The second diagram shows the variation used for the TD in week 17 and the big play in week 14. The counter action really sells the run away for the defense.

Why it Worked: Well timed play calling with excellent block out in front for the reverse man made this play go.

Why it Didn't Work: A holding call in week 2 brought the play back.

2 – Man Stick

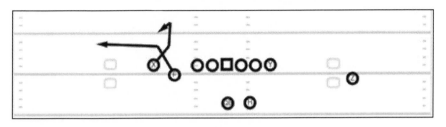

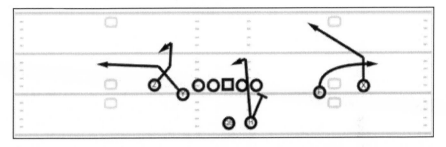

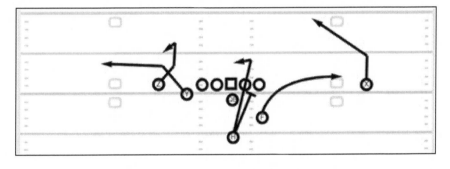

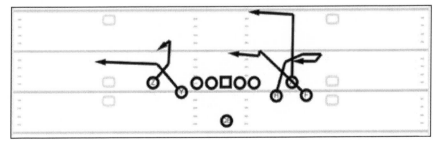

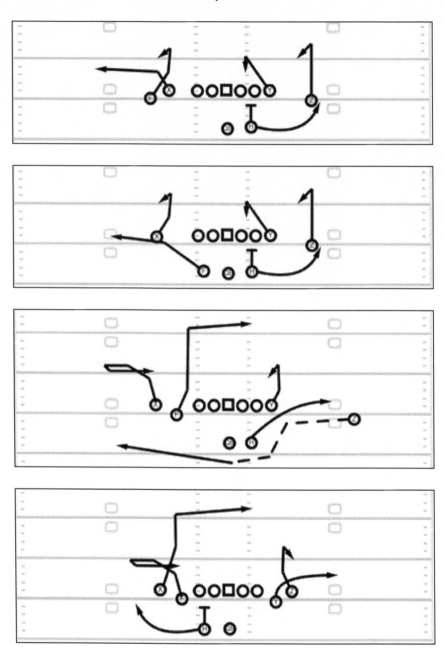

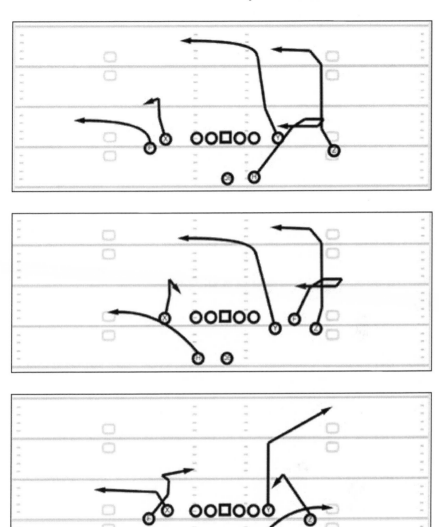

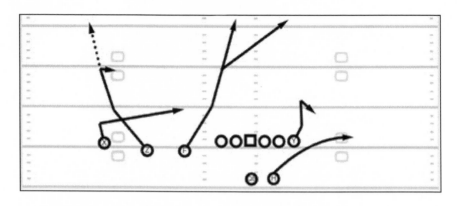

Average Yards per Play	4.1

1st Down		3rd/4th Down (includes RZ)	
Called	Average	Called	Success Rate
4	0.3	5	50%
2nd Down 6-1		2nd Down 7+	
Called	Average	Called	Average
3	9.0	2	5.5
Red Zone 10-0		Red Zone 10-20	
Called	Touchdown %	Called	Touchdown %
4	50%	1	0%

Cover 1		Cover 2		Cover 0	
Called	Average	Called	Average	Called	Average
3	8.3	3.0	-0.7	4.0	1.3
Cover 3		Cover 4			
Called	Average	Called	Average		
3	3.7	1	7.0		
Cover 5		Drop 8			
Called	Average	Called	Average		
2	8.0	0	0.0		

Week	Quarter	Time	Down	ToGo	Location	Yards
Week 2 vs CIN	1	6:38	1	10	SFO 16	0
Week 3 vs PIT	4	1:20	2	5	PIT 5	5
Week 8 vs CAR	3	0:36	3	6	CAR 6	0
Week 9 vs ARI	1	11:29	2	10	SFO 23	3
Week 10 vs SEA	1	11:13	1	10	SEA 40	-2
Week 13 vs BAL	4	6:33	4	1	RAV 35	0
Week 15 vs ATL	1	0:26	2	9	ATL 24	8
Week 16 vs LAR	1	10:52	1	10	RAM 18	9
Week 16 vs LAR	2	4:32	2	5	RAM 45	15
Week 16 vs LAR	4	14:10	2	5	SFO 11	7
Week 16 vs LAR	4	6:14	3	7	RAM 7	7
Week 16 vs LAR	4	2:30	1	10	SFO 25	-6
Week 17 vs SEA	3	3:25			SEA 2	0
DIV vs MIN	1	2:07	3	10	SFO 48	16
DIV vs MIN	4	11:11	3	4	SFO 20	0

Progression Read (front side concept)
1. Flat/Arrow
2. Stick
3. Back Side Combo

The 2 – man stick concept is a staple quick game concept throughout the NFL. The quick hitting element, and the horizontal stretch puts stress on a defense out of a compressed formation.

The 49ers often paired it with an in-breaking backside concept. These served as good options for the quarterback if the defense had the 2 man stick concept leveraged.

When paired with the dragon concept (slant-flat), the quarterback is taught to pick a side pre-snap. These versions are not pure progression reads.

The fourth diagram shows a low red zone variation used in weeks 3 and 8. The jerk route acts as a nice third option when defenses like to play the underneath routes aggressively to cover up the stick combination on the other side.

The 8th diagram was used a few times in week 16.

The coverage stats for this concept make sense from a theoretical standpoint. Against a hard-flat cover 2, the concept did not work as well.

The 11th diagram shows a low red zone variation used in week 17 for their 2 point conversion attempt. The jerk route from the stick runner is a nice way to get the double move on the front side of the concept.

Why it Worked: The long completion in week 16 shows Garoppolo getting to his third read quickly, and making a nice throw off-platform. These types of throws were common for Garoppolo throughout the season. One of his best skills is the ability to work through progressions quickly and making a nice throw without getting his feet set in place.

The touchdown in week 3 shows a well-timed throw to the stick route in the low red zone.

Why it Didn't Work: In week 2, the Bengals had a banjo call to the stick side, playing cover 2 underneath. Garoppolo threw to the covered flat route.

In the divisional round, the receiver dropped the ball on the "now slant" route (12th diagram).

3 – Man Stick

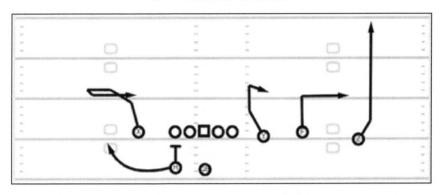

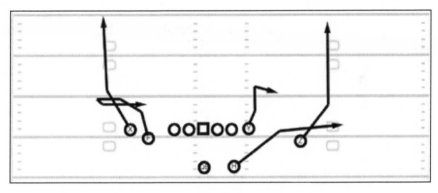

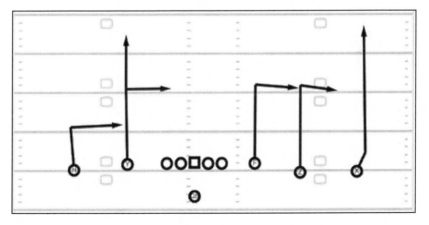

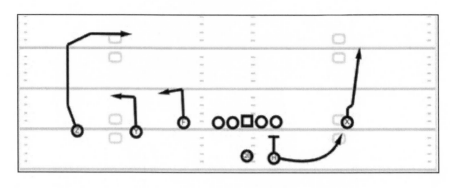

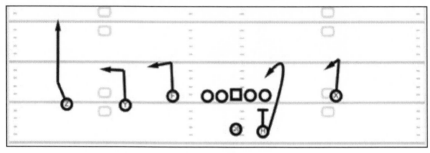

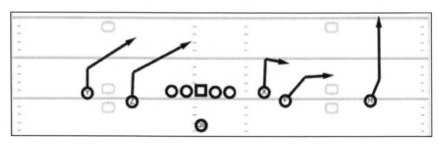

Average Yards per Play	5.2

1st Down		3rd/4th Down (includes RZ)	
Called	Average	Called	Success Rate
0	0.0	6	100%
2nd Down 6-1		2nd Down 7+	
Called	Average	Called	Average
2	5.0	1	5.0
Red Zone 10-0		Red Zone 10-20	
Called	Touchdown %	Called	Touchdown %
2	100%	0	0%

Cover 1		Cover 2		Cover 0	
Called	Average	Called	Average	Called	Average
7	5.3	0.0	0.0	0.0	0.0

Cover 3		Cover 4	
Called	Average	Called	Average
2	5.0	0	0.0

Cover 5		Drop 8	
Called	Average	Called	Average
0	0.0	1	5.0

Week	Quarter	Time	Down	ToGo	Location	Yards
Week 3 vs PIT	1	10:05	2	19	SFO 28	5
Week 6 vs LA	3	0:53	3	2	RAM 39	4
Week 7 vs WAS	3	0:05	3	8	SFO 43	13
Week 8 vs CAR	1	9:18	2	4	CAR 4	4
Week 9 vs ARI	2	3:17	3	6	CRD 40	7
Week 10 vs SEA	3	10:05	4	2	SEA 33	0
Week 10 vs SEA	4	1:31	3	5	SFO 31	5
Week 11 vs ARI	4	0:54	3	3	CRD 28	3
Week 14 vs NO	4	9:06	2	6	NOR 6	6

Progression Read (can be a dual read as well when paired with other quick game)

1. Outside Flat
2. Inside Stick
3. Back Side Combo

The 3 – man stick concept, similar to 2 – man stick, uses a quick hitting element, and the horizontal stretch puts stress on a defense.

This concept was a very efficient third & medium play call for the 49ers in 2019. The quick hitting nature prevents any blitz pressure from becoming a factor, and the out cuts are a safe throw if the ball is thrown accurately.

Why it Worked: Kittle made spectacular catches in week 7 and week 10. Great timing from Garoppolo allowed the 49ers to convert some key third downs with this concept. The double slant combination worked to convert in week 9, and the 2 man levels route converted in week 7.

Why it Didn't Work: A poor throw from Garoppolo resulted in the 4th down incompletion in week 10. The #2 receiver used nice technique to get open on this route.

Dragon

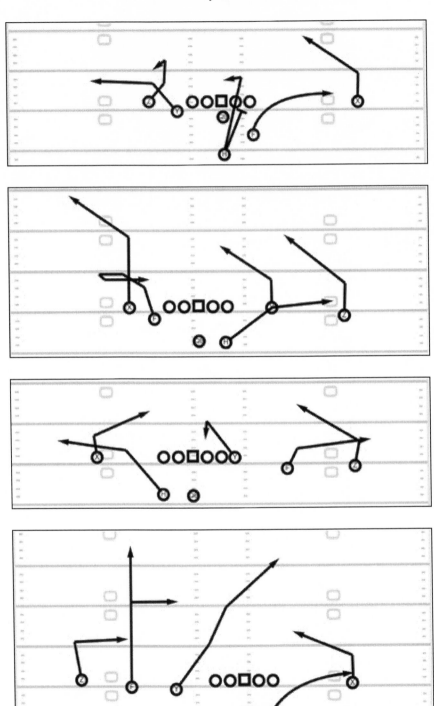

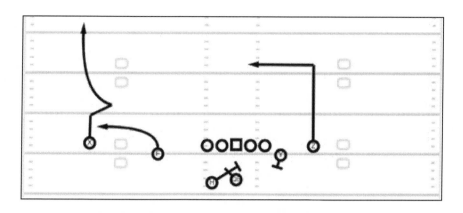

Average Yards per Play	4.1

1st Down		3rd/4th Down (includes RZ)	
Called	Average	Called	Success Rate
7	5.9	2	100%
2nd Down 6-1		**2nd Down 7+**	
Called	Average	Called	Average
3	0.0	7	3.7
Red Zone 10-0		**Red Zone 10-20**	
Called	Touchdown %	Called	Touchdown %
0	0%	2	0%

Cover 1		Cover 2		Cover 0	
Called	Average	Called	Average	Called	Average
6	8.0	2.0	0.0	0.0	0.0
Cover 3		**Cover 4**			
Called	Average	Called	Average		
7	3.9	2	-2.0		
Cover 5		**Drop 8**			
Called	Average	Called	Average		
4	-0.7	0	0.0		

Week	Quarter	Time	Down	ToGo	Location	Yards
Week 2 vs CIN	1	6:38	1	10	SFO 16	0
Week 6 vs LA	1	4:28	2	6	RAM 21	19
Week 7 vs WAS	3	12:41	4	4	WAS 36	TO
Week 9 vs ARI	1	11:29	2	10	SFO 23	3
Week 9 vs ARI	2	11:17	1	9	SFO 45	32
Week 9 vs ARI	2	3:20	2	6	CRD 40	0
Week 10 vs SEA	4	15:00	1	10	SFO 36	0
Week 10 vs SEA	4	10:22	1	10	SFO 31	4
Week 10 vs SEA	4	7:09	2	3	SEA 16	-5
Week 10 vs SEA	4	0:25	2	4	SEA 42	5
Week 10 vs SEA	OT	4:52	3	6	SEA 45	7
Week 11 vs ARI	4	1:09	1	10	CRD 35	0
Week 12 vs GB	2	6:11	1	10	SFO 32	18
Week 14 vs NO	4	9:52	2	8	NOR 14	0
Week 14 vs NO	4	6:06	1	10	SFO 25	5
Week 15 vs ATL	1	1:18	2	19	ATL 40	0
Week 16 vs LAR	2	3:10	2	7	RAM 27	11
Week 16 vs LAR	3	14:56	2	15	SFO 20	TO
Week 16 vs LAR	3	4:22	2	15	SFO 20	-2
DIV vs MIN	1	13:03	2	8	SFO 41	10
DIV vs MIN	1	2:55	1	10	SFO 48	0

Dragon is most often a dual read with a quick game concept opposite (slants, 2 man stick).

The Dragon concept has been around forever, and is a staple single high quick game concept. The slant and flat route put the flat defender in a bind.

The dragon concept was also attached to RPO's in week 10.

Running dragon on the backside of trips is a great way to attack "mable" coverage, where the defense pushes to the strength and leaves 2 on 2 to the weak side.

The sixth diagram shows a common 3 man version that was used. Against single high divider leverage, the #2 receiver has the inside track to get open on his slant route.

This can be seen in week 9 and the divisional round working against single high coverage.

The 8th diagram shows the version used twice in week 16. The route from the #3 receiver acts as the third read in the dragon progression if the hook defender stays low to help on the slant.

The double move was called in week 7.

Why it Worked: The concept worked as designed, and the 49ers picked up good yardage against single high coverages. The big play in week 9 shows how the 3 man version of this concept can work against single high coverage.

In week 10, the flat route opens up for a first down late in the game.

Why it Didn't Work: In week 16, the "Fin" route gets undercut from the levels concept. The double move call was intercepted by the free safety keying Garoppolo's eyes in week 7.

Bobby Peters

Slants

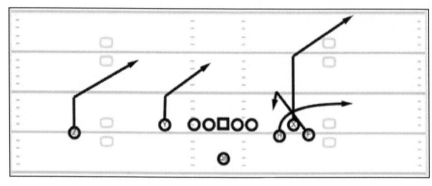

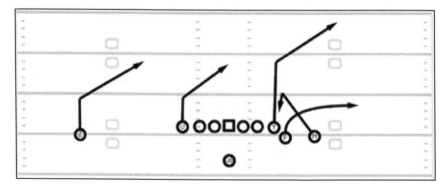

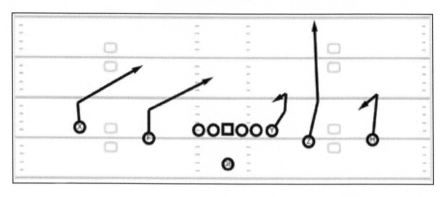

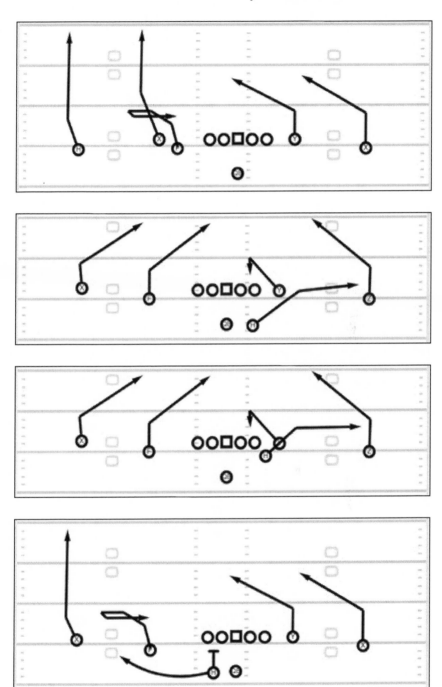

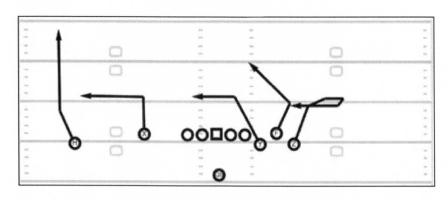

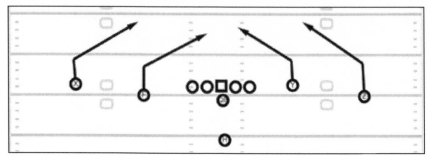

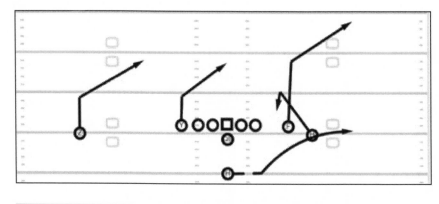

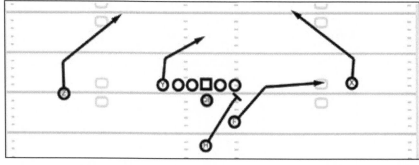

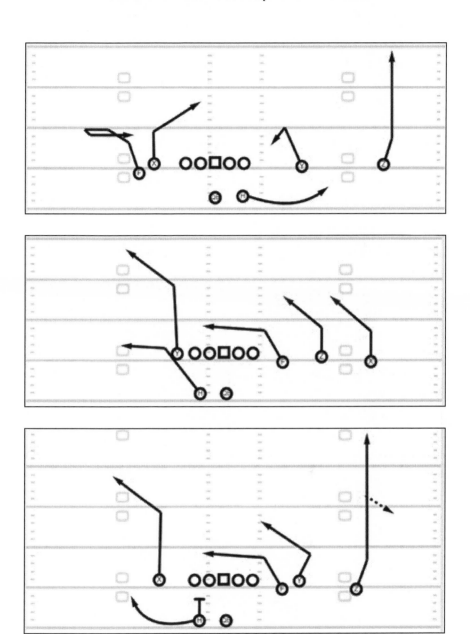

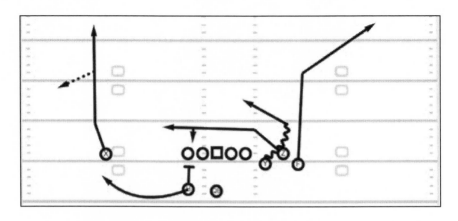

Average Yards per Play	6.3

1st Down		3rd/4th Down (includes RZ)	
Called	Average	Called	Success Rate
7	4.1	13	54%
2nd Down 6-1		**2nd Down 7+**	
Called	Average	Called	Average
2	2.5	10	5.0
Red Zone 10-0		**Red Zone 10-20**	
Called	Touchdown %	Called	Touchdown %
0	0%	1	0%

Cover 1		Cover 2		Cover 0	
Called	Average	Called	Average	Called	Average
9	5.6	4.0	5.0	0.0	0.0
Cover 3		**Cover 4**			
Called	Average	Called	Average		
10	8.0	5	5.8		
Cover 5		**Drop 8**			
Called	Average	Called	Average		
5	4.8	1	9.0		

Week	Quarter	Time	Down	ToGo	Location	Yards
Week 1 vs TB	2	10:29	3	12	SFO 6	14
Week 1 vs TB	2	8:47	2	18	SFO 12	TO
Week 3 vs PIT	**1**	**1:17**	**2**	**8**	**SFO 33**	**12**
Week 3 vs PIT	3	11:23	3	8	PIT 25	22
Week 5 vs CLE	1	8:33	1	10	CLE 27	3
Week 5 vs CLE	1	1:49	3	20	CLE 39	10
Week 5 vs CLE	4	5:16	3	7	CLE 26	0
Week 6 vs LA	4	13:35	2	10	RAM 24	9
Week 8 vs CAR	1	13:46	3	5	SFO 30	7
Week 9 vs ARI	1	2:22	2	4	CRD 42	0
Week 9 vs ARI	1	0:13	3	3	CRD 30	30
Week 9 vs ARI	2	3:17	3	6	CRD 40	7
Week 10 vs SEA	4	0:25	2	4	SEA 42	5
Week 10 vs SEA	OT	4:52	3	6	SEA 45	7
Week 11 vs ARI	**1**	**9:28**	**3**	**5**	**SFO 30**	**0**
Week 11 vs ARI	3	9:18	1	19	SFO 28	7
Week 11 vs ARI	3	8:39	2	12	SFO 35	5
Week 11 vs ARI	4	2:12	1	10	SFO 35	7
Week 11 vs ARI	4	1:09	1	10	CRD 35	0
Week 13 vs BAL	3	6:47	2	10	RAV 38	4
Week 13 vs BAL	3	0:17	3	4	SFO 7	12
Week 14 vs NO	2	1:54	1	13	NOR 35	7
Week 14 vs NO	4	6:06	1	10	SFO 25	5
Week 14 vs NO	**4**	**0:42**	**3**	**2**	**SFO 33**	**0**
Week 15 vs ATL	1	4:21	2	10	ATL 45	7
Week 15 vs ATL	1	1:18	2	19	ATL 40	0
Week 16 vs LAR	3	4:22	2	15	SFO 20	-2
Week 17 vs SEA	2	6:46	3	10	SEA 15	8
DIV vs MIN	1	13:03	2	8	SFO 41	10
DIV vs MIN	1	2:55	1	10	SFO 48	0
SB vs KC	**4**	**5:23**	**3**	**5**	**SFO 25**	**0**
SB vs KC	4	1:44	2	10	KAN 49	0

QB Read: Inside-Out

The double slant combination is great against many coverages. In cover two/palms, the outside receiver will typically have inside leverage.

Many of the concepts that the 49ers paired double slants with work well against single high coverage. Hoss, Scat, and Dragon.

The bolded clips are H Post variations. They were not used frequently enough for their own section.

Although they are not included in this section, the double slant concept works as an attached pass in RPO schemes. Against single high coverage, hitting the #2 receiver if the inside linebacker commits to his run gap is common for many NFL/college/high school teams.

Against two high shells pre-snap, I personally like slants paired with the scat/spot concept. With a cover 4 safety, the outside slant can become dangerous if he recognizes it quickly. When paired with scat/spot, the quarterback can read away from the middle linebacker's drop. If the middle linebacker follows the free release of the running back to the scat/spot side, the inside slant can hit vs cover 4 and the offense does not have to worry about a robbing safety. The 3Q 9:18 week 11 clip shows how this works against cover 4.

The empty hoss variations have this same effect. The QB can read away from the middle linebacker, and he will typically have a good idea pre-snap of which side he will read as well.

The 12th diagram shows a neat way of getting inside leverage for the outside slant route. Condensing the split and running a return route will create inside leverage. It will take a little longer to develop, however. This variation was used in week 15.

Why it Worked: The 49ers would often split Kittle out wide to run the outside slant. His big frame and catch radius make this a great usage of personnel for this concept. He made some nice plays throughout the season in this role. In week 9, Kittle lined up in the slot and had a nice 3rd down conversion on the slant route against cover 1 robber.

The concept had a very high success rate on 3rd/4th downs. Getting the ball out of the quarterbacks hands quickly eliminates the effectiveness of blitzes. Garoppolo has a lightning quick release, so the timing of the throw was typically on point as well.

Why it Didn't Work: In week 1, the corner picks off the hitch route on the hoss concept out of a single high look. Pettis drops a 3rd down attempt in week 5 on the outside slant. In week 17, the outside slant gets tackled right at the sticks just shy of converting a 3rd down.

In the late 3rd down in the Super Bowl, Garoppolo does not pull the trigger on the open H Post route (16th diagram).

Mini Jerk – Stutter Slant

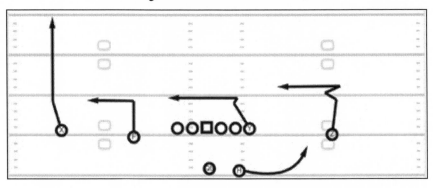

Week	Quarter	Time	Down	ToGo	Location	Yards
Week 3 vs PIT	3	1:39	2	8	PIT 16	12
Week 8 vs CAR	1	7:03	1	10	SFO 38	TO
Week 12 vs GB	2	6:11	1	10	SFO 32	18
Week 6 vs LA	1	4:28	2	6	RAM 21	19

Progression:
1. Flat – Fade Side
2. TE Mini Jerk
3. Stutter Slant
4. RB Swing

This concept acts like a quick game backside concept, similar to the Spacing concept. Typically paired with flat-fade, these routes open up into the quarterback's vision

The stutter slant route is found in a few concepts in Kyle Shanahan's offense. This route is meant to look like a sluggo at first. The receiver typically takes 3 steps vertical, 1 to the slant, 1 back vertical, then runs the final in-cut. These moves have a dual purpose. They are meant to create inside leverage vs an inside leverage corner, and to time up the window for the quarterback as a backside read.

Why It Worked: This play is a great way to get an athletic tight end like George Kittle in space on a linebacker. In week 12, the 49ers get cover 1 from GB. With the RB swinging away, the entire middle of the field is wide open, as the man defender was playing outside leverage on Kittle.

Garoppolo hits the flat route in week 6, but Kittle runs an awesome mini-jerk in this clip.

Why it Didn't Work: In week 8, Kittle drifts his route upfield. This allows Luke Kuechly to undercut the route for an interception.

Omaha

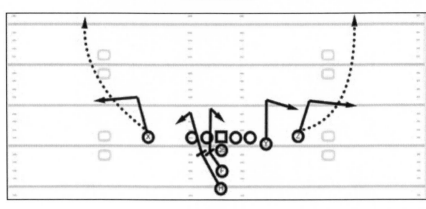

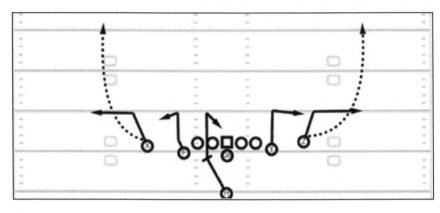

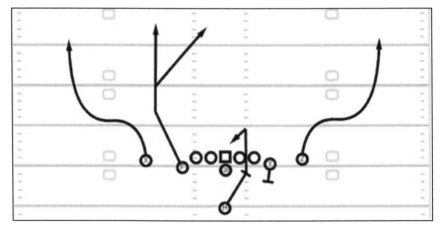

Average Yards per Play	8.4

1st Down		3rd/4th Down (includes RZ)	
Called	Average	Called	Success Rate
3	6.3	0	0%
2nd Down 6-1		**2nd Down 7+**	
Called	Average	Called	Average
2	18.0	2	2.0
Red Zone 10-0		**Red Zone 10-20**	
Called	Touchdown %	Called	Touchdown %
1	0%	0	0%

Cover 1		Cover 2		Cover 0	
Called	Average	Called	Average	Called	Average
1	0.0	1.0	4.0	0.0	0.0
Cover 3		**Cover 4**			
Called	Average	Called	Average		
5	11.0	1	4.0		
Cover 5		**Drop 8**			
Called	Average	Called	Average		
0	0.0	0	0.0		

Week	Quarter	Time	Down	ToGo	Location	Yards
Week 3 vs PIT	3	2:44	1	10	PIT 29	11
Week 5 vs CLE	3	14:59	1	10	SFO 10	8
Week 5 vs CLE	3	8:32	2	8	SFO 6	0
Week 8 vs CAR	1	14:26	2	9	SFO 26	4
Week 8 vs CAR	3	9:26	2	4	SFO 43	25
Week 11 vs ARI	2	8:03	1	4	CRD 4	0
Week 11 vs ARI	4	4:59	2	4	CRD 38	11

The Omaha route is a classic quick game concept in many NFL playbooks. A quick out from the condensed split is a great way to attack a soft cover 3 corner on a run down.

The critical coaching point is the receiver needs to press the outside hip of the defender to take away his angle at breaking on the route. This will also force him to retreat more and giving up more cushion for the Omaha route.

The outside route can convert to a fade vs press.

The double move shown in the third diagram is the big play from week 8.

Why it Worked: The double move hit big in week 8 against cover 3. The seam read route opened up and was not carried by an underneath defender.

Why it Didn't Work: A poor throw resulted in an incompletion in week 5. The Cardinals forced an incompletion in the low red zone by playing a catch technique on the goal line. By not pressing, the 49ers receivers did not run the adjusted fade route vs that look.

Hoss & Hoss Juke

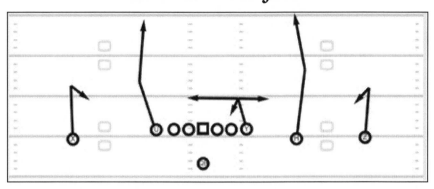

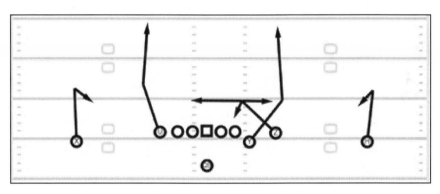

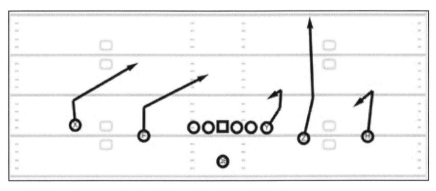

Week	Quarter	Time	Down	ToGo	Location	Yards
Week 1 vs TB	2	10:29	3	12	SFO 6	14
Week 1 vs TB	2	8:47	2	18	SFO 12	TO
Week 5 vs CLE	1	9:32	1	10	SFO 50	8
Week 10 vs SEA	3	1:42	1	10	SFO 25	8

While only used sparingly in 2019, this concept has been a part of Shanahan's system for years. The concept, when paired with the juke route or slants, is strong against any coverage or pressure. It gets the ball out of the QB's hands quickly.

The 2nd diagram shows a variation where the #2 and #3 receivers switch releases. This play was used in week 10.

The interception in week 1 was a result of a corner triggering on a hitch route out of a single high structure.

2 - Man Levels

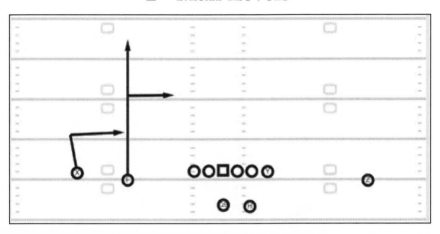

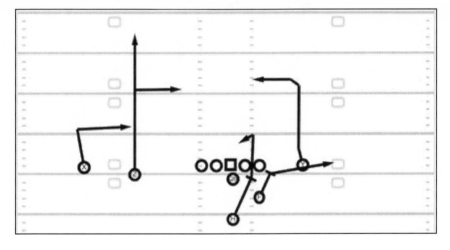

Bobby Peters

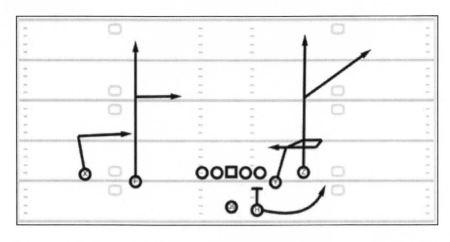

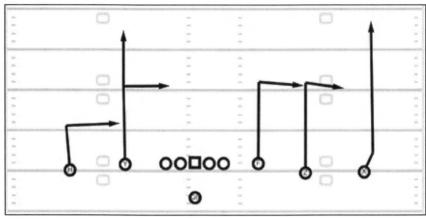

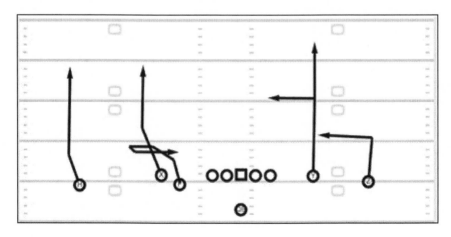

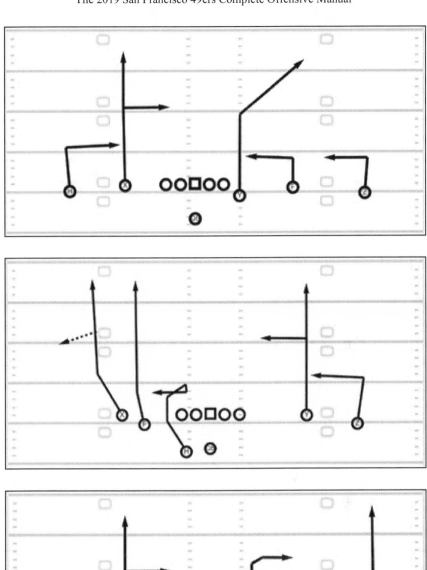

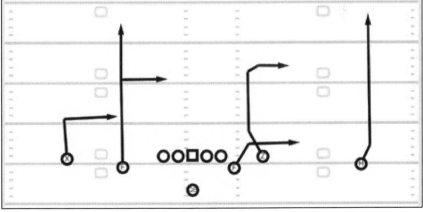

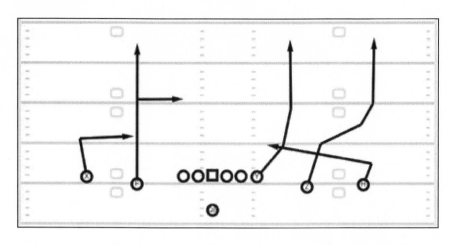

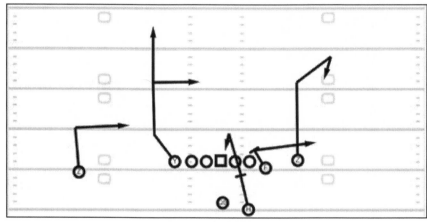

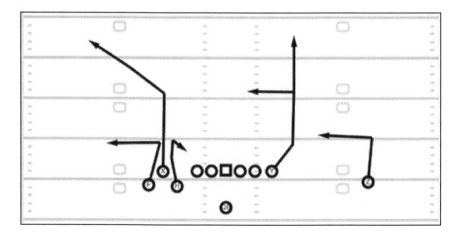

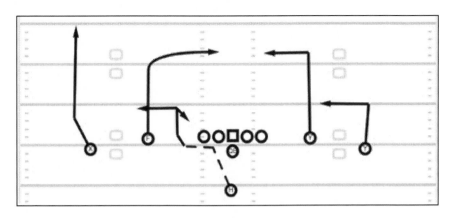

Average Yards per Play	5.2

1st Down		3rd/4th Down (includes RZ)	
Called	Average	Called	Success Rate
5	9.8	4	25%
2nd Down 6-1		**2nd Down 7+**	
Called	Average	Called	Average
3	10.0	8	2.0
Red Zone 10-0		**Red Zone 10-20**	
Called	Touchdown %	Called	Touchdown %
0	0%	1	0%

Cover 1		Cover 2		Cover 0	
Called	Average	Called	Average	Called	Average
5	8.4	6.0	6.5	1.0	5.0
Cover 3		**Cover 4**			
Called	Average	Called	Average		
5	2.6	2	0.0		
Cover 5		**Drop 8**			
Called	Average	Called	Average		
1	0.0	0	0.0		

Week	Quarter	Time	Down	ToGo	Location	Yards
Week 5 vs CLE	4	14:07	2	10	SFO 22	0
Week 6 vs LA	2	1:47	1	10	SFO 39	11
Week 7 vs WAS	3	0:05	3	8	SFO 43	13
Week 9 vs ARI	1	5:50	3	2	SFO 41	0
Week 10 vs SEA	4	1:39	1	10	SFO 26	0
Week 10 vs SEA	OT	1:46	2	10	SFO 20	0
Week 11 vs ARI	1	2:47	3	5	CRD 40	0
Week 12 vs GB	1	11:29	1	10	SFO 38	8
Week 12 vs GB	1	9:29	2	18	GNB 47	0
Week 12 vs GB	1	0:06	3	6	SFO 41	-7
Week 13 vs BAL	1	5:20	2	4	SFO 36	0
Week 13 vs BAL	3	4:29	2	13	RAV 19	5
Week 14 vs NO	1	9:54	1	10	NOR 30	25
Week 14 vs NO	3	13:36	2	11	SFO 35	TO
Week 14 vs NO	4	15:00	2	11	SFO 44	4
Week 14 vs NO	4	13:07	2	11	NOR 48	5
Week 14 vs NO	4	0:45	2	2	SFO 33	0
Week 15 vs ATL	4	12:26	1	10	SFO 28	5
DIV vs MIN	1	0:34	2	19	MIN 45	0
NFCCG vs GB	1	8:12	2	5	SFO 32	30

The two man levels concept, made popular by the Peyton Manning – led Colts and Broncos teams, is a great 2 high safety coverage beater. The "Fin" route (#1 on a 5 yard in cut) and the dig route from the #2 receiver place a high-low stretch on the weak hook defender.

Based on the patterns I've seen on film, I believe the route from the #2 receiver has the ability to stay vertical vs single high (no safety over the top) or to cut it off and run a dig at 10 yards vs 2 high safeties (help over the top). Against cover 3 match coverages, with outside leverage on the slot, this route would typically run the dig cut.

The 49ers game planned a new concept to pair with it on nearly a weekly basis. Typically, their menu of 3 man single high beaters were paired with it.

Using the 2 Man Levels concept in the context of a 1

high/2 high "pick a side" pairing allows the quarterback to get a post – snap read of any potential safety rotation. The 2 Man Levels Concept is not as quick hitting as traditional 3 step concepts. When running more typical "pick a side" quick game concepts, most post snap safety rotation goes undetected, and the defense often baits the QB into picking the wrong side.

The variations with the return route can be seen in weeks 6, 9, and 10 (4Q 1:39 & OT).

The variation with the H Whip tag (7th diagram) can be seen week 12 1Q 0:30.

The ninth diagram shows a variation with the "Glide" concept. This can be seen in week 13 3Q.

Why it Worked: A nice throw and catch converts on the dig route for a first down in week 7.

Why it Didn't Work: In general, the concept struggled for the 49ers against two high safety shells. In week 5, the middle linebacker get sunder the dig route in a cover 2 coverage in week 5. This forces Garoppolo off the concept at the top of his drop.

A contested throw to the "Fin" route results in a failed 3rd down conversion in week 9.

3 - Man Levels Variations

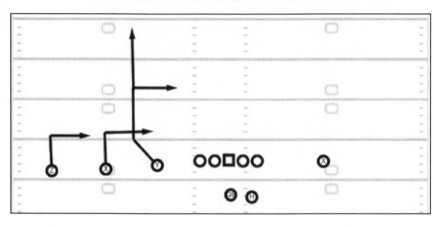

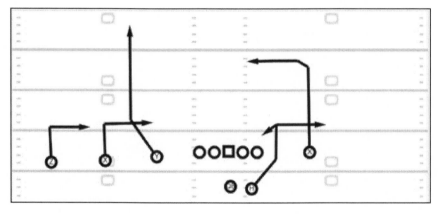

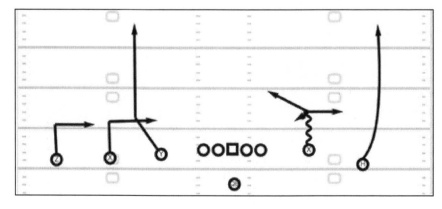

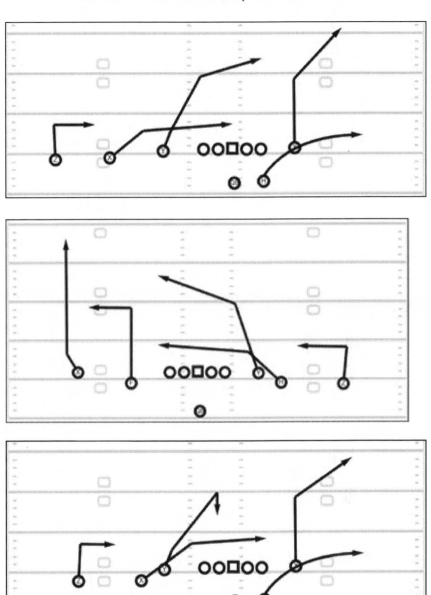

Average Yards per Play	6.9

1st Down		3rd/4th Down (includes RZ)	
Called	Average	Called	Success Rate
3	5.0	7	71%
2nd Down 6-1		**2nd Down 7+**	
Called	Average	Called	Average
0	0.0	3	5.5
Red Zone 10-0		**Red Zone 10-20**	
Called	Touchdown %	Called	Touchdown %
2	50%	0	0%

Cover 1		Cover 2		Cover 0	
Called	Average	Called	Average	Called	Average
5	8.2	1.0	7.0	2.0	4.0
Cover 3		**Cover 4**			
Called	Average	Called	Average		
4	6.8	1	0.0		
Cover 5		**Drop 8**			
Called	Average	Called	Average		
1	0.0	0	0.0		

Week	Quarter	Time	Down	ToGo	Location	Yards
Week 5 vs CLE	1	12:18	3	9	CLE 40	0
Week 6 vs LA	1	0:09	3	4	SFO 44	5
Week 8 vs CAR	3	7:59	3	6	CAR 28	8
Week 9 vs ARI	2	0:52	3	9	CRD 9	8
Week 10 vs SEA	1	2:07	3	8	SEA 10	10
Week 10 vs SEA	4	1:16	1	10	SFO 36	0
Week 11 vs ARI	4	4:47	2	7	CRD 24	0
Week 11 vs ARI	4	1:44	1	10	CRD 47	7
Week 16 vs LAR	2	3:10	2	7	RAM 27	11
Week 16 vs LAR	3	14:56	2	15	SFO 20	TO
Week 17 vs SEA	1	11:18	1	10	SFO 35	8
Week 17 vs SEA	1	3:26	3	5	SFO 11	5
Week 17 vs SEA	4	6:34	3	5	SEA 34	21

Progression Read (for first three diagrams):
1. Work Frontside Concept (Smash/Branch/ Weak Option/Bang Dig
2. #3 Vertical/Deep Dig
3. #2 Under
4. #1 Under

The 3 man levels concept is a staple ball control concept. It's a great way to get a high low read on a middle linebacker or strong hook defender. The 49ers like to keep #3 on a vertical up the seam against single high coverage.

The 49ers used a concept with #3 on a crossing route/search, with #2 on a drive route. These plays have been included in this section due to the similar areas of the field they attack. Good clips of these can be seen in week 17.

The second diagram shows a variation with a bang dig route. This variation slightly breaks the rules outlined in the progression read above. Both times this version was called, the #3 receiver to trips stayed vertical. The bang dig side is the read vs two high safeties. With #3 staying vertical, the levels side is the read vs single high. This version places the strong hook player in a high-low bind.

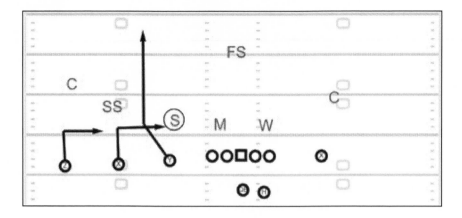

Why it Worked: Great route technique from Samuel in the long completion in week 17 on the corner route vs press coverage. The bang dig route was open both times it was called. Bourne wins on his drive route vs man coverage in week 10 for a TD.

Why it Didn't Work: The DB did a nice job of playing the receivers hands after the catch on the bang dig route in week 5. George Kittle gets tackled just short of the end zone vs an all out blitz in week 9. The Cardinals sack Garoppolo with a nice blitz in week 11. The drive route from #2 did not think he was getting the ball, so he slowed his route down in week 10. The drive would have opened up nicely against the cover 3 mable call from Seattle in this clip.

Branch

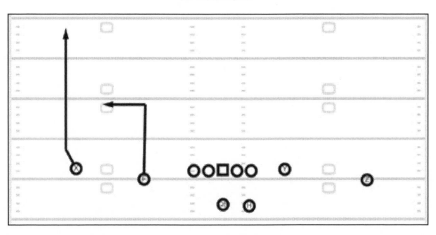

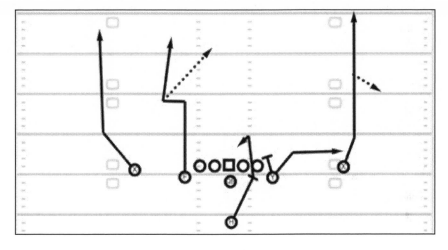

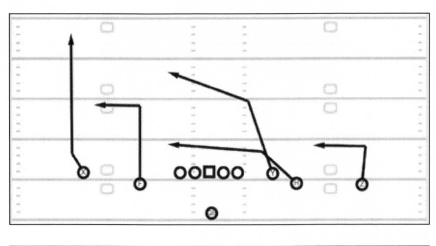

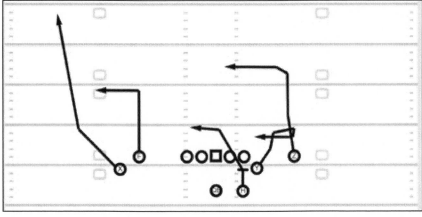

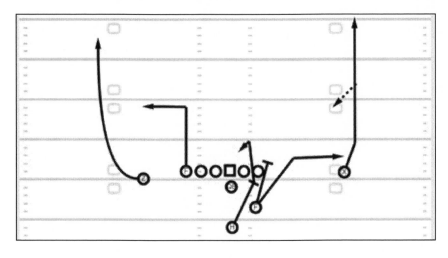

Average Yards per Play	8.4

1st Down		3rd/4th Down (includes RZ)	
Called	Average	Called	Success Rate
2	4.0	5	75%
2nd Down 6-1		**2nd Down 7+**	
Called	Average	Called	Average
0	0.0	2	14.5
Red Zone 10-0		**Red Zone 10-20**	
Called	Touchdown %	Called	Touchdown %
0	0%	0	0%

Cover 1		Cover 2		Cover 0	
Called	Average	Called	Average	Called	Average
3	11.0	0.0	0.0	0.0	0.0
Cover 3		**Cover 4**			
Called	Average	Called	Average		
6	7.2	0	0.0		
Cover 5		**Drop 8**			
Called	Average	Called	Average		
0	0.0	0	0.0		

Week	Quarter	Time	Down	ToGo	Location	Yards
Week 5 vs CLE	2	9:16	3	3	SFO 47	-7
Week 8 vs CAR	1	2:32	2	8	SFO 38	29
Week 9 vs ARI	3	7:47	3	4	CRD 46	22
Week 10 vs SEA	2	2:10	2	9	SFO 26	0
Week 11 vs ARI	1	2:43	4	5	CRD 40	0
Week 12 vs GB	4	10:04	3	10	SFO 31	13
Week 15 vs ATL	4	12:59	3	6	SFO 17	11
Week 17 vs SEA	1	11:18	1	10	SFO 35	8
DIV vs MIN	1	12:32	1	10	MIN 49	0

Branch is a common term used for a deep stick route paired with an outside fade. The concept is a great way to get bigger chunks with a similar action as the efficient stick concept. The branch route is typically the first read in the play that it is used with.

Another big benefit is against teams that like to trap the flat (think cover 2 of cover 5 cougar), the deeper out cut gives the QB an extra second to identify the trap.

Against cover 4, the 8 yard out cut pushes the boundary for the safety and his rules for identifying the #2 receiver as a vertical threat.

The double move variation can be seen in week 8 and week 10. These are bolded in the table.

The Branch concept was paired with the all curl concept. This combination is discussed in the All Curl section.

The fifth diagram shows a simple version that was used to get Kittle on the branch route.

Why it Worked: The double move call was open in week 8 and week 10. Both were against single high coverage and the double move stayed in the seam.

Why it Didn't Work: Tight coverage on the slot running the branch route allowed pressure to get home in week 5.

Smash Return

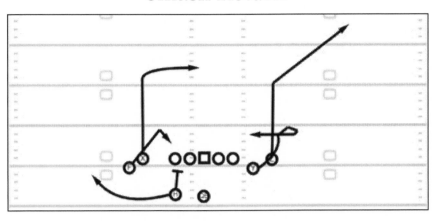

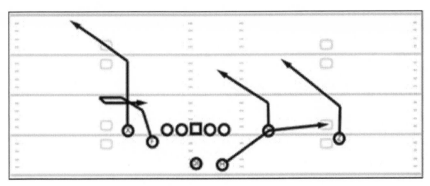

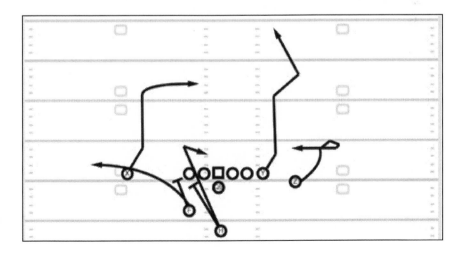

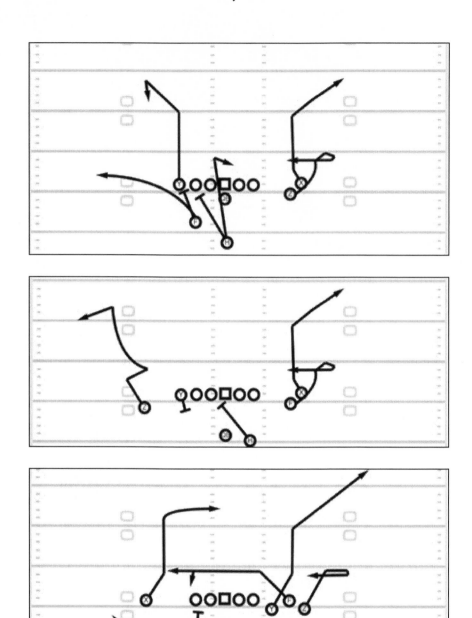

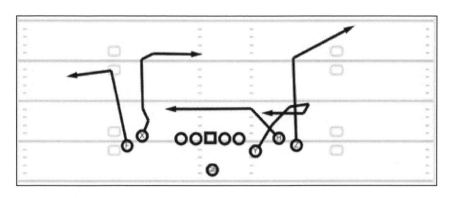

Average Yards per Play	6.5

1st Down		3rd/4th Down (includes RZ)	
Called	Average	Called	Success Rate
3	16.0	5	20%
2nd Down 6-1		**2nd Down 7+**	
Called	Average	Called	Average
2	0.0	1	7.0
Red Zone 10-0		**Red Zone 10-20**	
Called	Touchdown %	Called	Touchdown %
0	0%	1	0%

Cover 1		Cover 2		Cover 0	
Called	Average	Called	Average	Called	Average
4	13.8	2.0	0.0	0.0	0.0
Cover 3		**Cover 4**			
Called	Average	Called	Average		
5	2.5	1	0.0		
Cover 5		**Drop 8**			
Called	Average	Called	Average		
0	0.0	2	0.0		

Week	Quarter	Time	Down	ToGo	Location	Yards
Week 7 vs WAS	3	12:45	3	4	WAS 36	0
Week 9 vs ARI	2	11:17	1	9	SFO 45	32
Week 9 vs ARI	2	3:20	2	6	CRD 40	0
Week 9 vs ARI	4	7:06	2	12	SFO 31	7
Week 10 vs SEA	OT	1:50	1	10	SFO 20	0
Week 11 vs ARI	2	3:22	3	7	SFO 31	23
Week 12 vs GB	1	3:21	3	5	GNB 11	0
Week 13 vs BAL	2	0:15	2	4	RAV 36	0
Week 15 vs ATL	3	12:53	3	5	SFO 48	0
DIV vs MIN	2	2:49	1	10	SFO 19	TO
SB vs KC	3	10:28	3	5	KAN 27	3

Progression Read (most common)

1. Return Route
2. Corner Route
3. Backside concept

The Smash Return route is most often paired with a 3 man backside dig concept. When paired with other front side concepts (dragon, sock), the play is a dual read. The dragon version can be a read away from the weak hook defender in single high coverage.

The smash return concept is very versatile for the 49ers. The initial releases make it look like their often used weak side option call. It can be the front side of a progression read, and used in a dual read setting vs a certain look.

The concept works well against man coverages. Out of condensed sets, the return route gets a free release when it is run in the "jet stream" of the corner route. The man coverage defender has to chase over the top, and often loses the route after the 2nd cut. The key coaching point is the inside release of the corner route to force the inside defender from trailing the first cut from the #2 receiver.

This can be seen in week 11 as well as the image below.

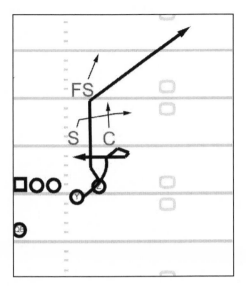

Against banjo calls, the return route will have inside leverage on the outside most defender. The corner will have to chase the return route from behind. This is shown in the week 10 clip and in the image below.

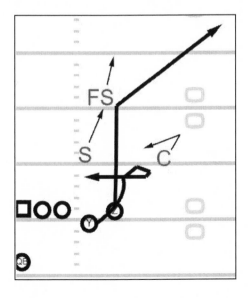

The 2nd diagram shows the concept being paired with 3 man dragon. Twice in week 9 against single high coverage, Garoppolo goes to the dragon side.

The 4th diagram shows a version where a swirl route is used as the backside route. This version can be seen late in the game in week 9.

The 5th diagram shows a max protection variation used in week 13 with a "Sock" (sluggo-stop) route. In this case, The smash return concept was paired in case the offense got two high coverage.

The 7th diagram shows the shallow variation used in week 15.

Why it Worked: The big play in week 9 was a slant to #2 in the 3 man dragon concept. The 49ers got a single high look, and Garoppolo correctly went to the other side of his dual read. In week 11, Garoppolo hits the corner route against man coverage.

Why it Didn't Work: In the divisional round, Garoppolo doesn't look at the flag side (paired with the Cop tag) and throws the backside dig into a spot dropping hook defender for an interception.

In week 12, the Packers flood out the zones by dropping 8 in the red zone.

Verticals & Variations (& PA)

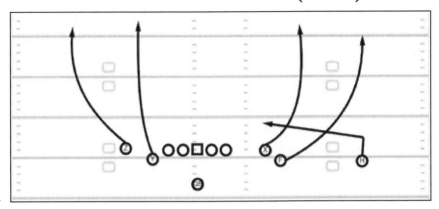

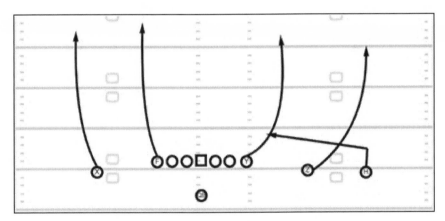

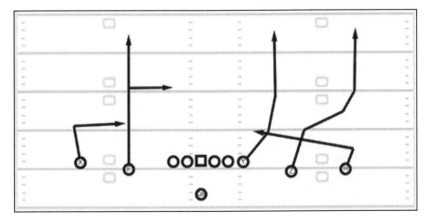

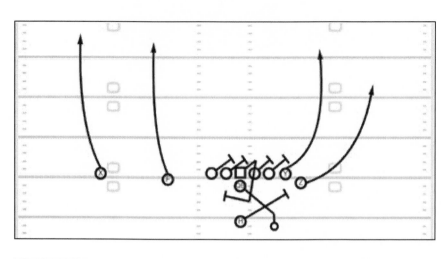

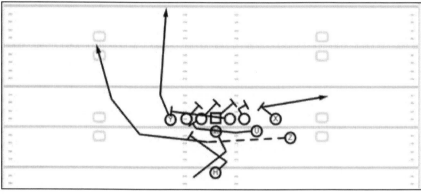

Average Yards per Play	6.9

1st Down		3rd/4th Down (includes RZ)	
Called	Average	Called	Success Rate
6	4.7	0	0%
2nd Down 6-1		**2nd Down 7+**	
Called	Average	Called	Average
1	13.0	7	7.9
Red Zone 10-0		**Red Zone 10-20**	
Called	Touchdown %	Called	Touchdown %
1	0%	4	0%

Cover 1		Cover 2		Cover 0	
Called	Average	Called	Average	Called	Average
1	0.0	3.0	8.3	1.0	5.0

Cover 3		Cover 4	
Called	Average	Called	Average
5	10.6	3	4.3

Cover 5		Drop 8	
Called	Average	Called	Average
0	0.0	2	12.5

Week	Quarter	Time	Down	ToGo	Location	Yards
Week 1 vs TB	3	13:26	2	10	SFO 37	0
Week 2 vs CIN	2	0:11	1	10	CIN 15	0
Week 2 vs CIN	3	13:11	2	1	CIN 16	13
Week 5 vs CLE	1	7:09	1	9	CLE 9	0
Week 6 vs LA	3	6:39	2	9	RAM 23	21
Week 7 vs WAS	2	2:42	1	10	SFO 42	0
Week 9 vs ARI	1	6:30	2	11	SFO 32	9
Week 9 vs ARI	2	1:35	2	13	CRD 13	4
Week 11 vs ARI	3	1:07	1	10	CRD 48	19
Week 11 vs ARI	4	5:39	1	10	CRD 44	6
Week 11 vs ARI	4	4:55	1	10	CRD 27	3
Week 13 vs BAL	3	4:29	2	13	RAV 19	5
Week 15 vs ATL	3	1:24	2	12	SFO 46	16
DIV vs MIN	1	0:34	2	19	MIN 45	0

The first three diagrams show the vertical concept with a drive route coming from #1 in trips. With many teams playing versions of "stubbie" coverage to three receiver surfaces, this version is a way to get the singled up outside receiver more involved in the play. In most cases, the outside vertical to the wide side of the field tends to be an afterthought. Shanahan pairs it with his 2 – man levels concept as well to have another option for his quarterback against 2 high shells.

Play action is a great way to get to vertical concepts as well.

This was not a big part of the 49ers offense, but the couple that were used are included in this section.

Why it Worked: In week 6, Garoppolo throws a well-timed pass into the seam of the LA Rams cover 3 spot drop zone. In week 2, Garoppolo hits the drive route coming under the mike linebacker in a two high shell.

Why it Didn't Work: In week 1, the ball seems to get lost in the sun and is slightly overthrown.

Weak Side Option with Stick – Nod

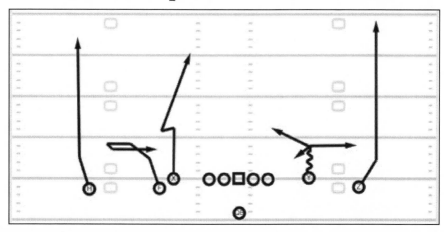

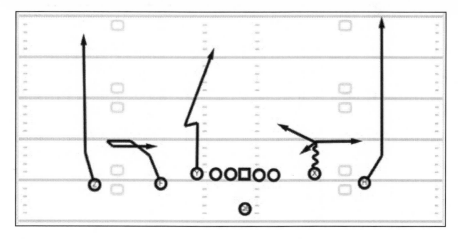

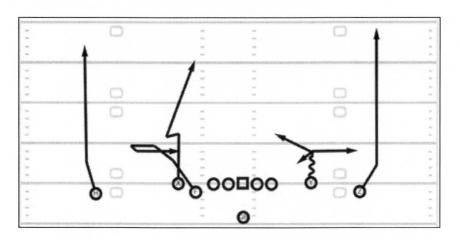

Average Yards per Play	13.0

1st Down		3rd/4th Down (includes RZ)	
Called	Average	Called	Success Rate
1	7.0	2	100%
2nd Down 6-1		**2nd Down 7+**	
Called	Average	Called	Average
0	0.0	3	6.7
Red Zone 10-0		**Red Zone 10-20**	
Called	Touchdown %	Called	Touchdown %
0	0%	0	0%

Cover 1		Cover 2		Cover 0	
Called	Average	Called	Average	Called	Average
1	6.0	2.0	9.0	0.0	0.0
Cover 3		**Cover 4**			
Called	Average	Called	Average		
2	23.5	1	7.0		
Cover 5		**Drop 8**			
Called	Average	Called	Average		
0	0.0	2	7.0		

Week	Quarter	Time	Down	ToGo	Location	Yards
Week 1 vs TB	2	5:51	1	10	TAM 31	7
Week 1 vs TB	4	4:42	2	10	SFO 25	6
Week 5 vs CLE	3	8:30	3	8	SFO 6	11
Week 7 vs WAS	3	8:48	3	3	SFO 30	40
Week 9 vs ARI	1	0:54	2	10	CRD 37	7
Week 13 vs BAL	2	10:43	2	10	SFO 45	7

Progression Read:
1. Weak Side Option
2. Stick Nod
3. Return

Pairing the stick nod concept with the weak side option route gives the quarterback a nice full field progression read. The concept is strong against all coverages and blitzes. The weak side option route gives the quarterback a quick throw against a free rusher

In two high coverage shells, when the defense wants to get 3 over 2 weak and trap the option route, the stick nod is 1 on 1 with a linebacker.

In single high structures that bracket the option route, the stick nod and return route high-low the strong hook player. Against man coverages, the option route can win vs a given leverage, and the stick nod is a nice double move to shake free.

Why it Worked: Garoppolo hit the weak side option route five times for completions, against many different coverages (including drop 8). Richie James ran a wicked stick nod route in week 7 for a big gain.

Why it Didn't Work: The concept worked great for the 49ers in 2019.

Weak Side Option with Return Route

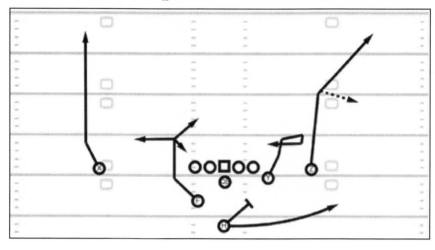

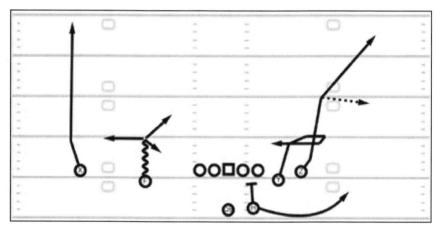

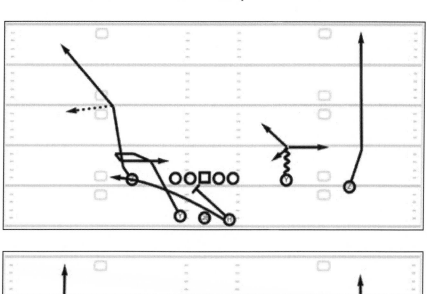

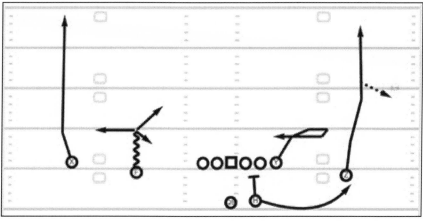

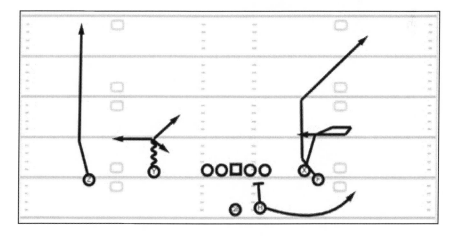

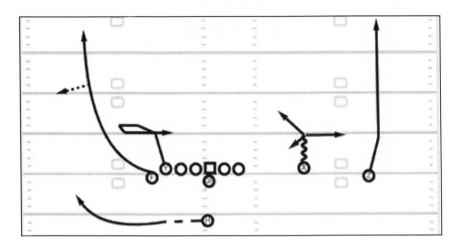

Progression (6-man protection variation):
1. Alert Corner/Fade vs trapping CB
2. Weak Side Option Route
3. Return Route
4. Check-Release Swing

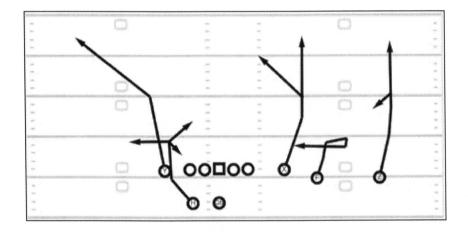

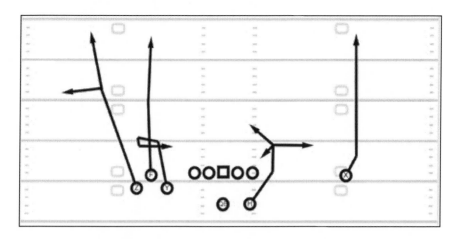

Progression (Seam on Return side):
1. Alert Corner/Fade vs trapping CB
2. Weak Side Option Route
3. Seam Read
4. Return Route

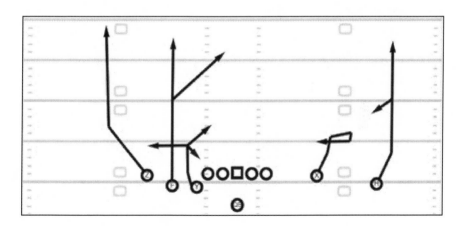

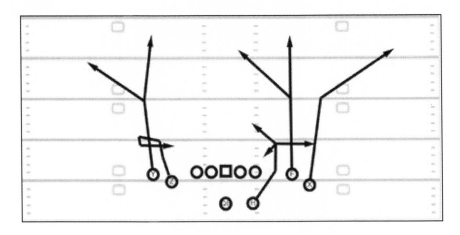

Progression (#3 Option Route)
1. Alert Croner/Fade vs trapping CB
2. Seam Read
3. Option Route
4. Return Route

Average Yards per Play	8.1

1st Down		3rd/4th Down (includes RZ)	
Called	Average	Called	Success Rate
5	11.2	6	67%
2nd Down 6-1		**2nd Down 7+**	
Called	Average	Called	Average
1	8.0	2	7.5
Red Zone 10-0		**Red Zone 10-20**	
Called	Touchdown %	Called	Touchdown %
2	50%	0	0%

Cover 1		Cover 2		Cover 0	
Called	Average	Called	Average	Called	Average
4	11.3	4.0	3.8	2.0	15.0

Cover 3		Cover 4	
Called	Average	Called	Average
4	6.0	0	0.0

Cover 5		Drop 8	
Called	Average	Called	Average
0	0.0	1	2.0

Week	Quarter	Time	Down	ToGo	Location	Yards
Week 3 vs PIT	2	10:37	1	10	PIT 49	8
Week 3 vs PIT	4	5:29	1	10	PIT 24	9
Week 5 vs CLE	1	6:30	3	5	CLE 5	5
Week 7 vs WAS	1	0:54	3	7	SFO 49	11
Week 7 vs WAS	3	0:38	2	7	SFO 44	-1
Week 8 vs CAR	3	4:41	3	5	CAR 40	-8
Week 9 vs ARI	4	6:18	3	5	SFO 38	2
Week 10 vs SEA	4	1:10	2	10	SFO 36	16
Week 11 vs ARI	4	0:37	1	10	CRD 25	25
Week 15 vs ATL	2	13:39	3	4	ATL 7	5
Week 16 vs LAR	2	3:49	1	10	RAM 30	3
Week 16 vs LAR	3	13:19	2	4	SFO 48	8
DIV vs MIN	1	11:40	1	10	MIN 27	11
SB vs KC	2	0:20	3	5	SFO 25	20

With the option route being a staple concept in the 49ers offense, tagging the return route as a back side route creates an easy progression for the quarterback, while flooding the underneath zones. If the defense squeezes the option route, the inside defender vacating his zone will leave extra room for the return route. In man coverage with a bracket on the option route runner, the return route should be able to win vs his defender.

The 49ers have the ability to run both the option route and the return route to a three man side as well. When running either concept to the three man side, they will have the additional receiver run a seam read route. This addition slightly changes the progression in each version.

Against teams that like to trap the flats aggressively out of two high, I like the seam read on the side of the option route. This gets the option route on the middle linebacker, without the help of a trapping corner.

I like the seam read on the side of the option route against single high cover 3 teams as well. Divider leverage and rules dictate the option route will be isolated on the strong hook player. If the weak hook player cheats over to help on the option route, the return route will have inside leverage on his route. The play is draw below.

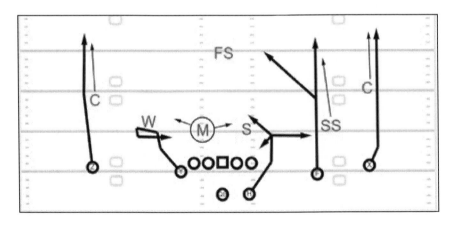

Why it Worked: In week 11, the 49ers win the game with this concept. The Cardinals bring a zero pressure, and Wilson runs an excellent option route out of the backfield for the 25 yard score. With an unblocked rusher coming at him, Garoppolo makes an outstanding throw.

In general, Garoppolo's quick release pairs perfectly with

the weak side option route. A majority of the clips shows him hitting this route on time right out of the break. This route requires a quick release, as the quarterback has to react to which cut the option route runner makes.

Why it Didn't Work: In week 9, the Cardinals drop 8 and trap the flat on the option route. The 49ers get the completion, but the corner makes a nice tackle to prevent the first down.

In week 7, Washington plays cover 3. They are able to get inside-out leverage on the option route, and pass off the return and RB check swing. The sloppy conditions don't help the offense on this play either.

Weak Side Option with Spot – Dig

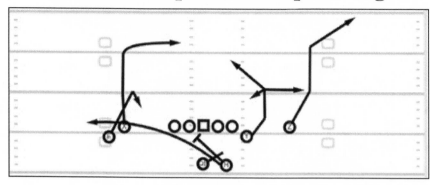

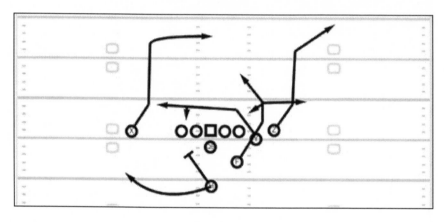

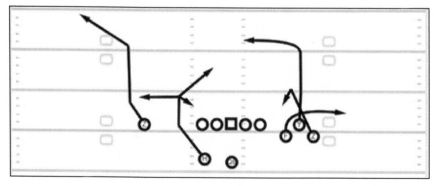

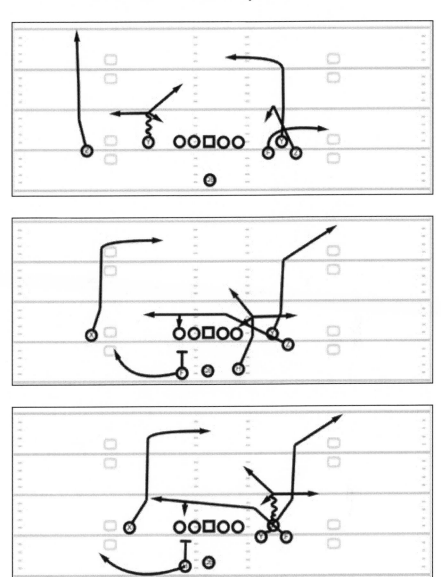

Average Yards per Play	10.3

1st Down		3rd/4th Down (includes RZ)	
Called	Average	Called	Success Rate
3	5.7	5	50%
2nd Down 6-1		**2nd Down 7+**	
Called	Average	Called	Average
0	0.0	1	13.0
Red Zone 10-0		**Red Zone 10-20**	
Called	Touchdown %	Called	Touchdown %
1	0%	0	0%

Cover 1		Cover 2		Cover 0	
Called	Average	Called	Average	Called	Average
1	8.0	1.0	0.0	0.0	0.0

Cover 3		Cover 4	
Called	Average	Called	Average
6	7.7	0	0.0

Cover 5		Drop 8	
Called	Average	Called	Average
1	39.0	1	13.0

Week	Quarter	Time	Down	ToGo	Location	Yards
Week 6 vs LA	2	2:23	3	6	SFO 5	11
Week 8 vs CAR	2	8:12	3	11	SFO 44	13
Week 9 vs ARI	1	4:30	1	10	SFO 41	9
Week 11 vs ARI	2	0:39	1	20	CRD 26	0
Week 11 vs ARI	3	6:11	2	18	CRD 25	13
Week 12 vs GB	2	3:03	3	2	GNB 9	0
Week 13 vs BAL	1	12:44	3	2	RAV 33	0
Week 14 vs NO	4	0:39	4	2	SFO 33	39
SB vs KC	4	2:02	1	15	SFO 27	8

Progression
1. Alert Fade/Corner vs trapping CB
2. Weak Side Option Route

3. Dig
4. Drag/Spot
5. Check Wide

The Spot – Dig backside combination gives the quarterback a high-low read if the defense brackets/squeezes the option route. In single high structures, the spot – dig concept gives the offense a 3 over 2 on the strong side of the formation if the defense double teams the option route. A great clip of this can be seen in the week 8 third down conversion. This stretch is shown below.

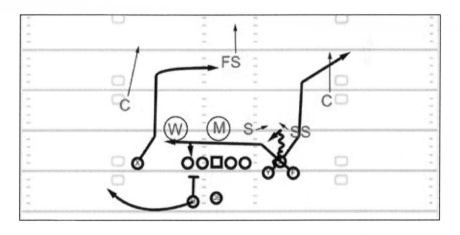

The sixth diagram shows the version used for the big 4th down conversion in week 14. This variation is a great way to get a free release on the option route against tight man coverage.

Sometimes the 49ers will tag the option route runner on a locked out route. These clips are included in this section as well for convenience. By my eye, I only spotted 3.

Why it Worked: George Kittle converts a huge 4th down

off the option route in the 4Q of the Saints game.

Garoppolo is able to hit the option route against cover 3 in week 6. The flat defender expands to try and get under a potential underneath route from #1.

Why it Didn't Work: In week 12, Garoppolo tries to force it into the option route in the low red zone, when he could have gotten off to the back side dig for a touchdown. This one is hard to pin on the QB though, as this happens real fast in the low red zone.

A poor throw in week 13 to the open back side dig results in a tough catch opportunity that falls incomplete.

On 3rd down in week 13, the Ravens bracket the backside dig with the free safety in a fire zone cover 3 coverage. The coverage ends up looking like a "box" check to the bunch. The Spot – Dig combination can be covered up with a "box" check when run out of a 3 man bunch.

Misc. Option Routes and Constraints

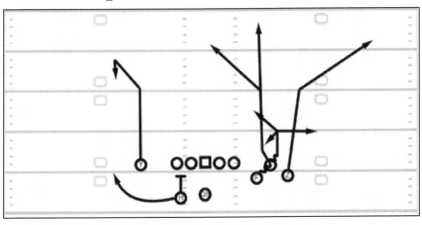

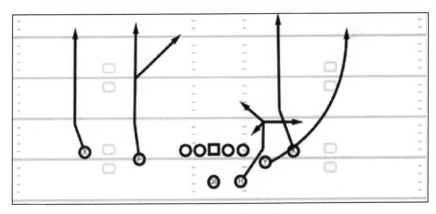

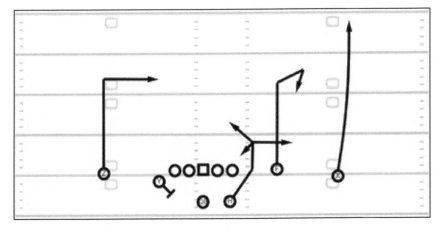

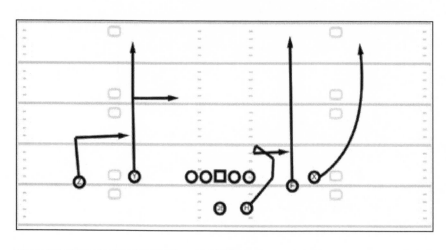

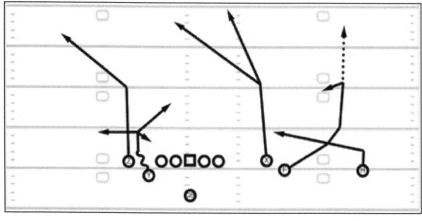

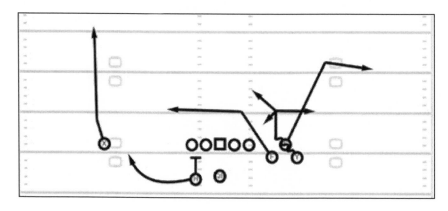

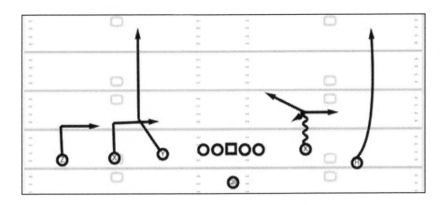

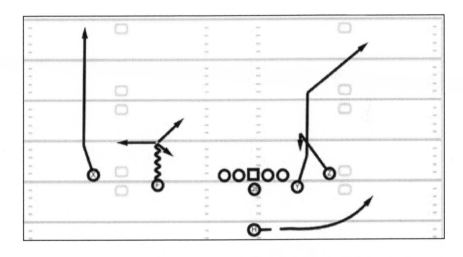

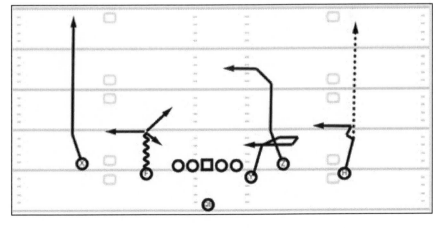

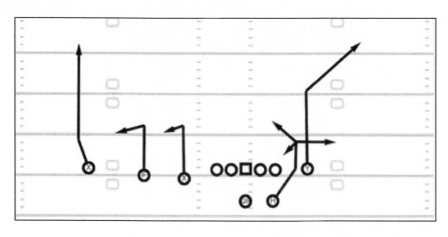

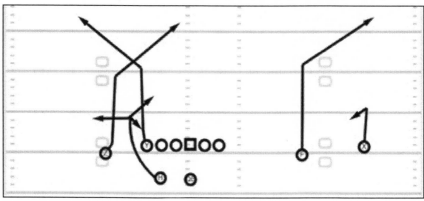

Average Yards per Play	5.3

1st Down		3rd/4th Down (includes RZ)	
Called	Average	Called	Success Rate
2	8.0	6	50%
2nd Down 6-1		2nd Down 7+	
Called	Average	Called	Average
1	14.0	4	4.8
Red Zone 10-0		Red Zone 10-20	
Called	Touchdown %	Called	Touchdown %
0	0%	2	0%

Cover 1		Cover 2		Cover 0	
Called	Average	Called	Average	Called	Average
4	5.3	1.0	3.0	1.0	5.0

Cover 3		Cover 4	
Called	Average	Called	Average
3	5.0	5	5.6

Cover 5		Drop 8	
Called	Average	Called	Average
0	0.0	1	0.0

Week	Quarter	Time	Down	ToGo	Location	Yards
Week 1 vs TB	1	11:55	2	15	TAM 18	0
Week 1 vs TB	3	14:23	3	8	SFO 27	10
Week 1 vs TB	3	2:46	3	10	TAM 39	0
Week 1 vs TB	4	4:00	3	4	SFO 31	5
Week 6 vs LA	2	1:53	1	10	SFO 27	12
Week 8 vs CAR	3	5:19	2	10	CAR 45	5
Week 9 vs ARI	2	10:08	1	10	CRD 11	4
Week 9 vs ARI	3	14:06	3	6	SFO 32	9
Week 10 vs SEA	1	10:27	2	12	SEA 42	12
Week 11 vs ARI	2	1:23	2	6	CRD 30	14
Week 11 vs ARI	2	0:35	2	20	CRD 26	2
Week 12 vs GB	1	0:06	3	6	SFO 41	-7
Week 13 vs BAL	1	5:16	3	4	SFO 36	3

Kyle Shanahan has been creative with how he packages the underneath option route over the years. He will most commonly pair it with the concepts discussed in previous sections (return route, spot dig, stick nod). This section is to discuss the lesser used versions.

I have an affinity for unique combinations and constraints for the underneath option route. There is a certain aesthetic to them being executed, backyard football-esque. Getting the matchup, creating the free release, etc.

The first 4 diagrams show the unique ways he used the option route to the 3 man side.

The 4th diagram shows the whip route from the backfield in week 12. Paired with 2 – man levels, this play has answers for all coverages.

The sixth diagram shows a way to get the option route from the #1 receiver in the bunch. Against "point/traffic" and "lock and level", the option route will typically break in or sit with this version. This one was used in week 1 with Kittle running the option route.

The 7th diagram shows how the concept can be paired with the 3 – man levels combination. With the option route being good against 2 high safeties, the 3 – man levels with a locked seam from #3 is a nice single high compliment. The intricacies of 3 – man levels are broken down in that section.

The 11th diagram shows a cool version used in week 1. Combining Scissors with the choice route is a great 3 man concept against most coverages and blitzes. The scissors action is a great way to take a shot with the post route trailing the tight end's release against quarters coverage. Tampa Bay plays quarters here, but Garoppolo doesn't take a shot at the open post route.

Why it Worked: Creative concepts with matchups in mind usually create success for an offense over time. The option route is a staple route in the system, so these creative uses don't require a ton of new teaching.

Why it Didn't Work: Quick pressure in week 12 did not allow for the whip route to time up. A poor throw in week 1 prevented a 3rd down conversion.

Bang Dig with Return Route

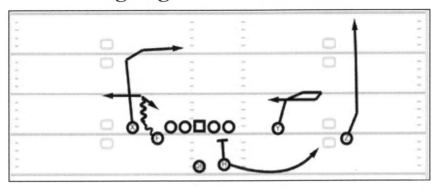

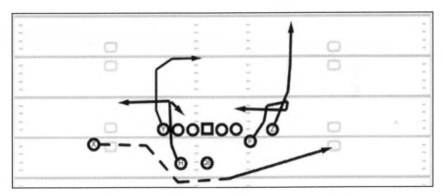

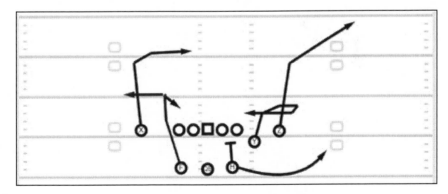

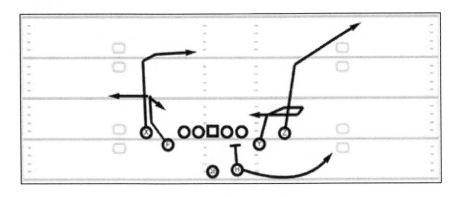

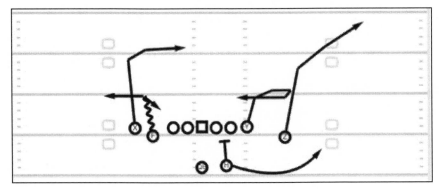

Progression (6-man protection variation):
1. Bang Dig (Sit/Out vs LB depth)
2. Return Route
3. Check-Release Swing

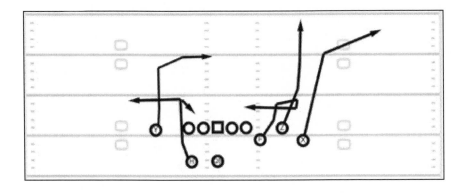

Progression (Seam on Return side):
1. Bang Dig (Sit/Out vs LB Depth or robbing cover 4 safety)
2. Seam Read
3. Return Route

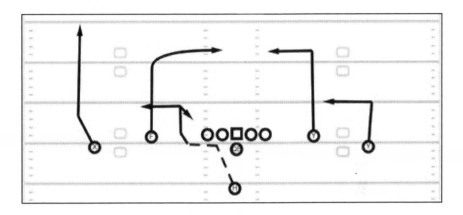

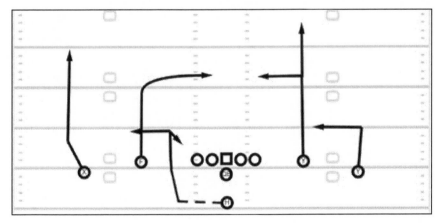

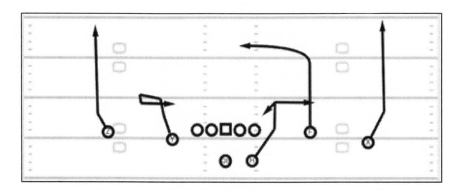

Split Field Progression Read (#2 Strong on Bang Dig):
1. Read Bang Dig side vs single high
2. Read levels/return side vs two high

Average Yards per Play	10.7

1st Down		3rd/4th Down (includes RZ)	
Called	Average	Called	Success Rate
4	8.8	7	71%
2nd Down 6-1		2nd Down 7+	
Called	Average	Called	Average
4	20.5	3	9.0
Red Zone 10-0		Red Zone 10-20	
Called	Touchdown %	Called	Touchdown %
0	0%	1	0%

Cover 1		Cover 2		Cover 0	
Called	Average	Called	Average	Called	Average
5	9.8	3.0	17.3	0.0	0.0

Cover 3		Cover 4	
Called	Average	Called	Average
7	12.2	3	-1.5

Cover 5		Drop 8	
Called	Average	Called	Average
1	5.0	1	11.0

Week	Quarter	Time	Down	ToGo	Location	Yards
Week 2 vs CIN	2	1:09	1	10	SFO 44	0
Week 3 vs PIT	2	9:59	2	2	PIT 41	15
Week 3 vs PIT	2	9:11	3	6	PIT 22	11
Week 3 vs PIT	4	2:47	2	17	PIT 20	6
Week 9 vs ARI	3	3:03	2	7	SFO 42	12
Week 9 vs ARI	4	2:00	3	9	CRD 48	11
Week 10 vs SEA	3	10:56	2	6	SEA 37	-5
Week 10 vs SEA	4	6:26	3	8	SEA 21	0
Week 11 vs ARI	4	4:41	3	7	CRD 24	TO
Week 12 vs GB	2	1:05	2	6	GNB 42	42
Week 14 vs NO	1	9:54	1	10	NOR 30	25
Week 14 vs NO	3	13:36	2	11	SFO 35	TO
Week 14 vs NO	3	0:56	1	10	SFO 45	5
Week 14 vs NO	4	12:25	3	6	NOR 43	6
Week 14 vs NO	4	11:01	3	5	NOR 32	16
Week 15 vs ATL	4	12:26	1	10	SFO 28	5
Week 16 vs LAR	3	8:41	3	5	SFO 49	-8
NFCCG vs GB	1	8:12	2	5	SFO 32	30

This concept has a lot of carry over with the Weak Side Option – Return concept, as it is meant as a constraint. The Quarterback will key the quick dig combination (instead of the weak option).

Based on film, it appears that the choice route only has two options on this play. The ability for this receiver to break in is taken away in order to keep the hook window clear for the dig route.

If the defense aggressively covers up the weak side option with underneath defenders, the dig route can slip behind them and hit quick for a big gain. The diagram below shows how the defense can bracket the underneath route, opening up the dig window. If the opposite hook defender cheats (circled defender), the return route will open up.

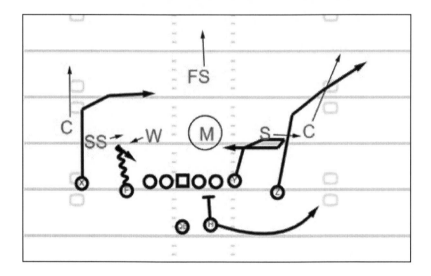

Against two high safeties, the quarterback will read away from the middle linebacker's drop. With three receiving threats going the opposite way, the QB will typically end up on the side of the bang dig. With cover 4 safeties being able to rob the dig, the quarterback will then work to his second progression (the sit/out) The image below shows the window vs cover 2, and the following image shows the bracket on the dig vs cover 4 (option route 1 on 1 with LB).

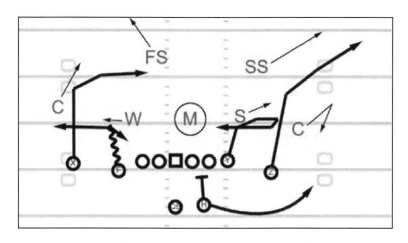

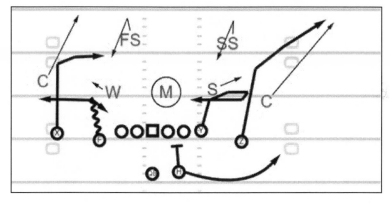

Using the Bang dig to the three receiver surface has particular advantages and acts as a nice changeup for the base version. The last diagram shows the variation that went for a touchdown in week 12 vs GB. The Packers played a pattern match cover 3, which has the defender over the slot play with outside leverage. With the running back free releasing into his option route, the inside hook defender must honor him as the "fast 3". With outside leverage on the dig cut and no inside help, the 49ers had a well designed play go to the house. The image below shows how this concept can carve up single high coverage

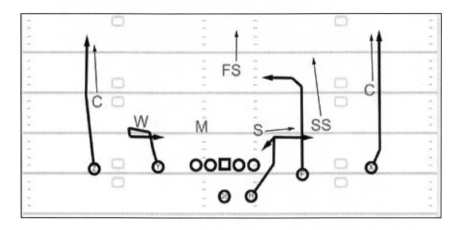

Why it Worked: The concept worked like a charm in week 14, converting back to back third downs. In the first clipm the Saints play "lock and level" to the 2-man bunch and press the point. The sit/out worked his free release to the outside and created a nice window for Garoppolo. The Saints brought a 6 man pressure here as well.

The 2nd conversion in week 14 was against a fire zone blitz. The Saints played cover 3, with outside leverage on the bunched receivers. Garoppolo hits the bang dig for a big play.

Against two high coverage, Garoppolo worked the 2 – man levels concept in the 7th diagram in the NFCCG. This clip is great teaching tape.

Why it Didn't Work: On 1Q week 14, the running back runs his sit/out option route to the wrong side.

In week 16, the Rams play cover 4 and bracket the bang dig. The sit/out option is played with tight inside leverage. The pressure gets to Garoppolo before he has a chance to set up for the return route.

In week 2 and week10, the receiver drops a well-timed throw on the bang dig.

Stick – Nod with #1 Now Slant

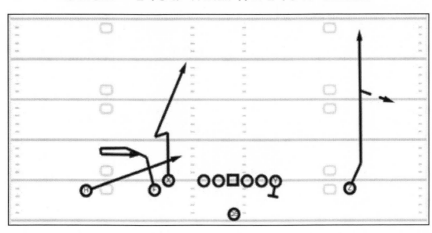

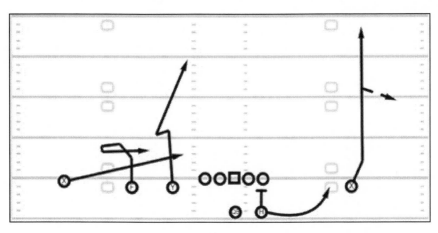

Cover 1		Cover 2		Cover 0	
Called	Average	Called	Average	Called	Average
1	0.0	1.0	3.0	1.0	0.0

Cover 3		Cover 4	
Called	Average	Called	Average
3	12.7	0	0.0

Cover 5		Drop 8	
Called	Average	Called	Average
0	0.0	0	0.0

Average Yards per Play	6.8

1st Down		3rd/4th Down (includes RZ)	
Called	Average	Called	Success Rate
1	14.0	2	0%
2nd Down 6-1		2nd Down 7+	
Called	Average	Called	Average
0	0.0	3	9.0
Red Zone 10-0		Red Zone 10-20	
Called	Touchdown %	Called	Touchdown %
0	0%	1	0%

Week	Quarter	Time	Down	ToGo	Location	Yards
Week 1 vs TB	4	2:24	3	8	TAM 29	0
Week 3 vs PIT	3	7:23	3	5	SFO 30	0
Week 11 vs ARI	2	8:38	1	10	CRD 18	14
Week 13 vs BAL	1	14:22	2	10	SFO 26	3
Week 13 vs BAL	4	13:20	2	18	SFO 24	8
SB vs KC	4	1:56	2	7	SFO 35	16

Progression Read

1. Now Slant (#1 receiver)
2. Stick Nod (#3 receiver)
3. Return (#2 receiver)

Although used sparingly in 2019, this concept has been successful for Shanahan over the years.

The play is similar to the popular stick nod concept, with one small adjustment. Against tampa 2 coverages where the middle linebacker won't bite on the stick fake, the now slant will come open underneath. The image below shows the play.

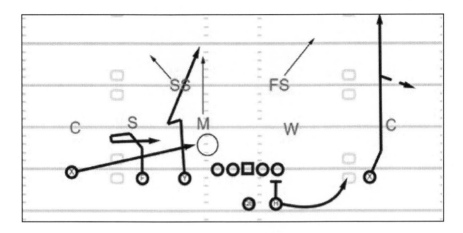

The now slant is also the read for the quarterback if he is faced with all out pressure.

Why it Worked: In week 11, the now slant works under the mike and picks up a good gain in the red zone.

Why it Didn't Work: In week 1, the Bucs bring quick A gap pressure, and force Garoppolo to throw the now slant into man coverage. The defender is playing with inside leverage and takes the route away.

In week 3, the Steelers play a 1 Robber variation and are able to bracket the now slant and play the stick nod with outside leverage. Against this coverage, the return route should be able to work open with leverage being played outside by the man defender.

In general, the 49ers routes were not crisp. In particular, the stick nod route.

All Curls (& Front Side Tags)

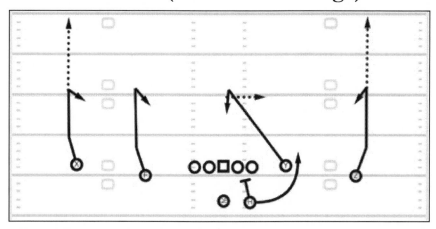

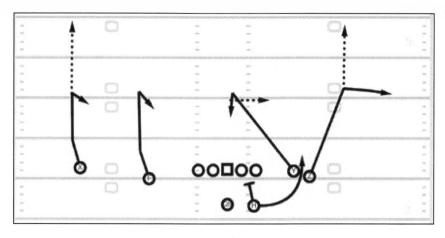

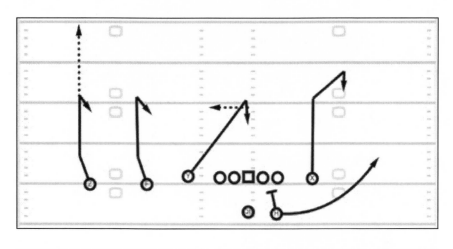

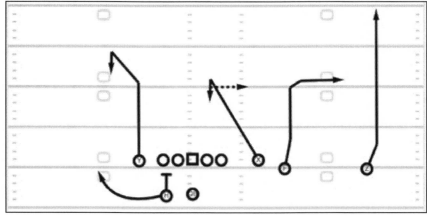

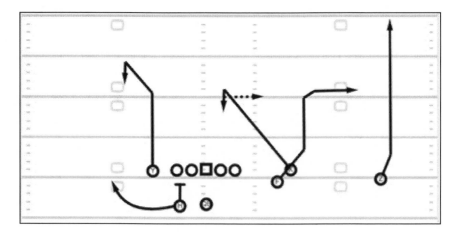

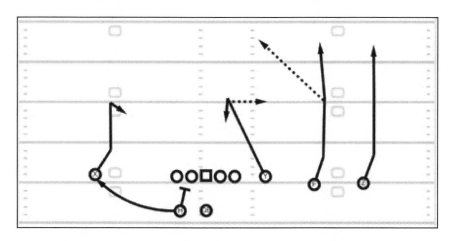

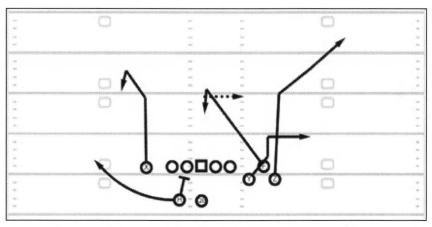

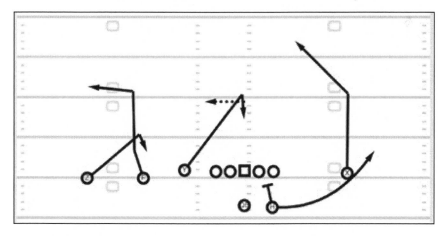

Average Yards per Play	7.8

1st Down		3rd/4th Down (includes RZ)	
Called	Average	Called	Success Rate
1	22.0	8	38%

2nd Down 6-1		2nd Down 7+	
Called	Average	Called	Average
0	0.0	3	8.0

Red Zone 10-0		Red Zone 10-20	
Called	Touchdown %	Called	Touchdown %
0	0%	3	0%

Cover 1		Cover 2		Cover 0	
Called	Average	Called	Average	Called	Average
3	6.3	4.0	8.0	0.0	0.0

Cover 3		Cover 4	
Called	Average	Called	Average
3	13.3	2	4.0

Cover 5		Drop 8	
Called	Average	Called	Average
1	0.0	0	0.0

Week	Quarter	Time	Down	ToGo	Location	Yards
Week 10 vs SEA	4	1:36	2	10	SFO 26	0
Week 11 vs ARI	3	2:09	2	17	SFO 18	8
Week 12 vs GB	2	0:24	1	10	SFO 48	22
Week 12 vs GB	4	10:04	3	10	SFO 31	13
Week 13 vs BAL	2	10:03	3	3	RAV 48	8
Week 13 vs BAL	3	6:05	3	6	RAV 34	5
Week 14 vs NO	4	9:44	3	8	NOR 14	2
Week 15 vs ATL	3	1:24	2	12	SFO 46	16
Week 15 vs ATL	4	12:59	3	6	SFO 17	11
Week 16 vs LAR	3	11:24	3	6	RAM 40	2
NFCCG vs GB	2	2:10	3	8	GNB 15	6
SB vs KC	1	8:07	3	5	KAN 20	0

Progression (All Curl Variation)
1. Alert: Outside Hinge/Out vs 1 on 1 Favorable Matchup/Leverage.
2. Middle Curl
3. Work Inside – Out Away From Pressure

Progression Read (Tagged Variations)
1. Tagged Concept (Branch/Smash/Bender)
2. Search Route
3. Swirl/Curl
4. RB Check Down

The All Curl concept is a great drop back pass concept against any coverage. Against two high, the 49ers would often get George Kittle isolated on an inside linebacker on the "search" route between the hashes. Against single high coverage when the defense brackets the middle hook, the 1 on 1's can be found in the slot or on the outside.

The 49ers did a nice job of adapting the true All Curl concept with a couple different 2 man concepts. The Branch concept (Fade – 10 Yard Out), a vertical bender, and a condensed smash variation were all used in 2019. The Branch variation (diagrams 4 and 5) were common and effective 3rd down variations. Against single high looks, the branch route would open up and cut under the seam players' outside leverage.

The concepts that were tagged were typically game-planned against the third down defense they were seeing that week. If they didn't get the anticipated look, the had a nice backside triangle read with the search-swirl-check down that works against any coverage.

Why it Worked: the third down conversion vs SEA in week 17 is an awesome clip of throwing the search route open vs tight 1 on 1 coverage. Kittle worked back to the outside and Jimmy Garoppolo threw it with great anticipation. Kittle also caught a search route on 2nd down in week 15 vs a tampa 2 look.

The Branch route opened up in week 12 and week 15 3rd down. This route is a great tag vs an outside leverage seam player in a cover 3 match coverage.

Why it Didn't Work: Against a "stubbie" look from the Saints in week 14, the search route was not able to open up. The swirl route got jammed off the line of scrimmage, and the Rams did a nice job of converging on the search route with their inverted cover 2 in week 16.

Z Curl – Hank Drop Back Variations

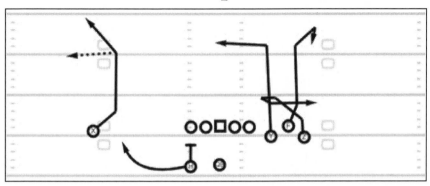

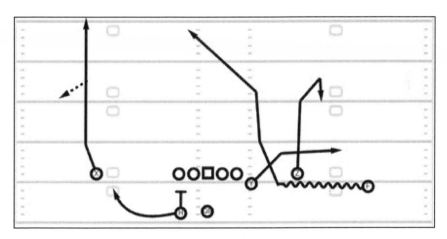

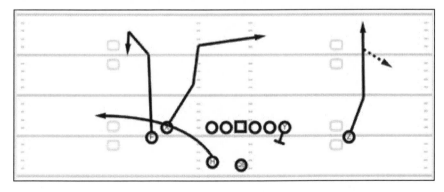

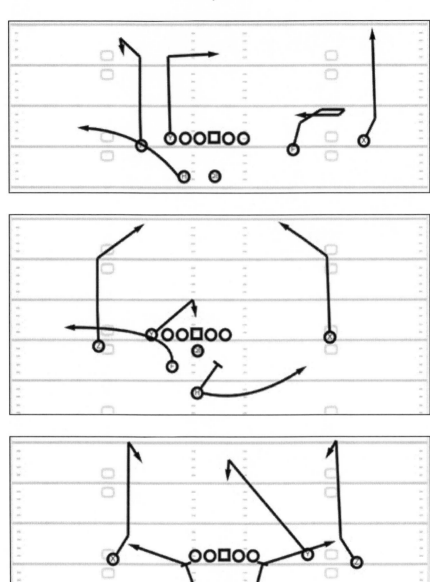

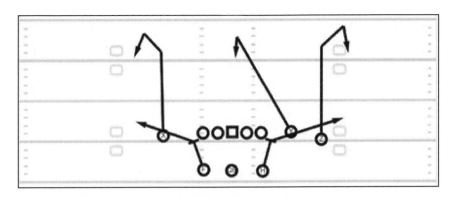

Average Yards per Play	7.6

1st Down		3rd/4th Down (includes RZ)	
Called	Average	Called	Success Rate
1	19.0	12	64%
2nd Down 6-1		**2nd Down 7+**	
Called	Average	Called	Average
0	0.0	1	7.0
Red Zone 10-0		**Red Zone 10-20**	
Called	Touchdown %	Called	Touchdown %
2	50%	0	0%

Cover 1		Cover 2		Cover 0	
Called	Average	Called	Average	Called	Average
4	9.8	1.0	16.0	1.0	7.0
Cover 3		**Cover 4**			
Called	Average	Called	Average		
2	17.5	6	1.5		
Cover 5		**Drop 8**			
Called	Average	Called	Average		
1	7.0	1	17.0		

Week	Quarter	Time	Down	ToGo	Location	Yards
Week 6 vs LA	3	8:06	3	6	RAM 35	11
Week 7 vs WAS	1	5:59	3	9	SFO 30	9
Week 7 vs WAS	3	6:15	3	5	WAS 10	0
Week 9 vs ARI	4	8:34	3	11	SFO 16	17
Week 9 vs ARI	4	4:37	3	11	SFO 25	16
Week 10 vs SEA	1	8:29	3	5	SEA 25	0
Week 10 vs SEA	2	10:39	1	10	SFO 8	19
Week 11 vs ARI	4	1:05	2	10	CRD 35	7
Week 14 vs NO	1	8:31	3	6	NOR 6	6
Week 14 vs NO	1	3:22	3	12	SFO 23	-9
Week 15 vs ATL	3	6:04	3	11	ATL 35	7
Week 16 vs LAR	4	1:57	3	16	SFO 19	18
DIV vs MIN	2	11:39	3	12	SFO 45	14
SB vs KC	4	1:33	4	10	KAN 49	-9

The Z-Curl action is another way to get to the curl/flat read. The key difference here is the vertical stem from the #2 receiver. This route will hold any quarters safety from robbing the #1 receiver on his curl route, as he has to carry the vertical stem of #2.

The first diagram shows a constraint version of Z Curl meant to look like the drive concept. This version is also designed to give defenses fits that make "lock and level" or "point/traffic" checks. In these coverages, with the immediate drive release of the #1 receiver, the outside corner will have to commit hard to fighting through/over the top to get into position to defend the drive route. This is enough of a distraction to free up the whip cut from the #1 receiver. A great clip of this can be seen in week 6. With Aaron Donald bearing down on him, Garoppolo makes a great throw to pick up the first down. The image below shows the tough responsibility of the corner.

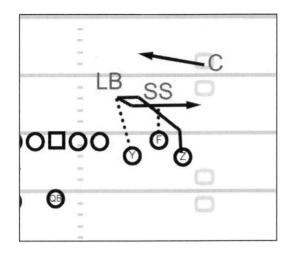

A "Swirl" route is commonly used within this concept as a substitute for the traditional curl route. A "Swirl" is a curl route from a condensed split, meant to mimic the top of a corner route. This is a nice compliment if you run a lot of smash concepts.

The 3rd diagram shows a variation with the back free releasing, and the tight end staying in the protection. This version was used in week 11 and the divisional round.

Although not used as commonly as Z-Curl, Hank was a part of the 49ers 3rd and long package. Typically used with bumps from the running backs to help the tackles before the get into their check down routes.

Why it Worked: Garoppolo made some nice throws in week 9 to pick up some 3rd and longs late in a close game. Climbing the pocket to find a receiver who works back to the ball are critical components for picking up these long yardage situations. The bumps from the running backs help give the quarterback more time to throw as well.

In week 14, Garoppolo hits the swirl route in the low red zone for a touchdown. The Saints play a quasi-"box" coverage to the concept. The image below shows how the swirl route worked to get inside leverage on the deep outside defender.

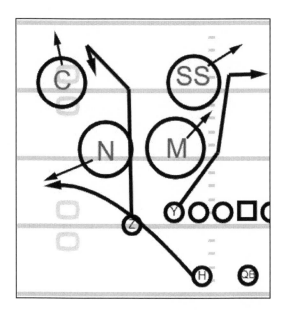

Why it Didn't Work: In week 10, Seattle's corner does a nice job recovering on the whip route. Garoppolo then sails a sails on the swirl route.

In week 15, the Falcons play a coverage that looks like "box" as well. The flat/1st out defender gets more depth, being a third and 11. This significantly tightens the window to the swirl route. Garoppolo hesitates, and the interior pass rush gets to him.

Double Digs/Drop Back Y Cross

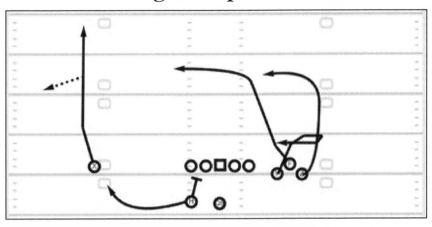

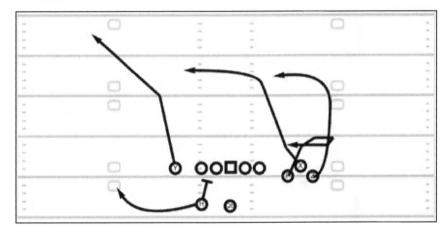

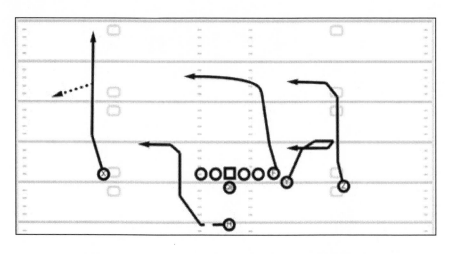

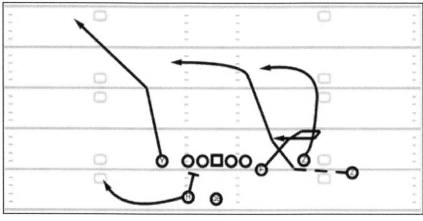

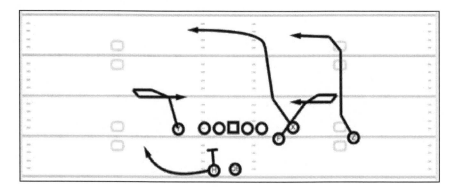

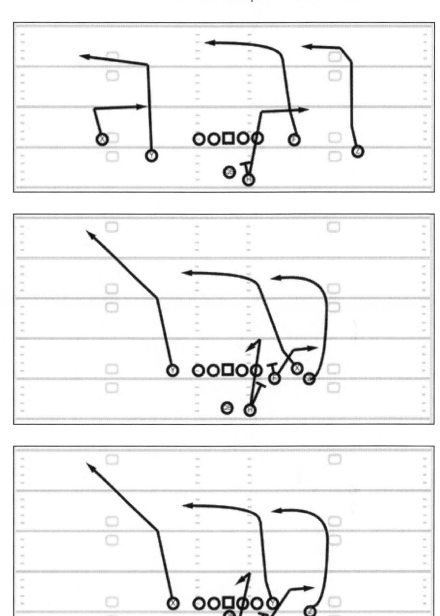

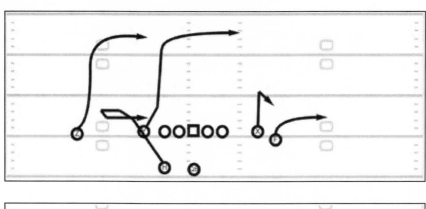

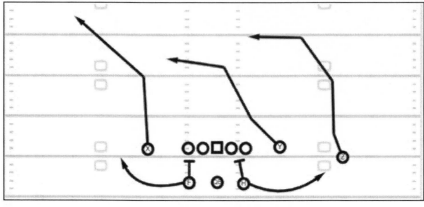

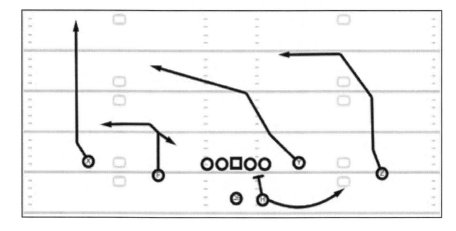

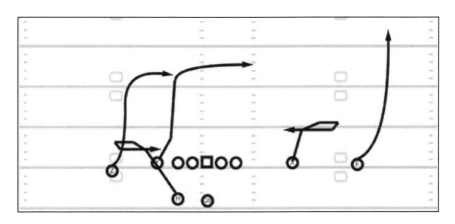

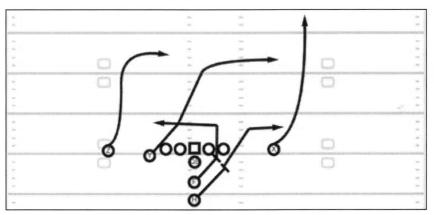

Average Yards per Play	7.0

1st Down		3rd/4th Down (includes RZ)	
Called	Average	Called	Success Rate
5	5.2	12	50%
2nd Down 6-1		**2nd Down 7+**	
Called	Average	Called	Average
1	5.0	2	2.0
Red Zone 10-0		**Red Zone 10-20**	
Called	Touchdown %	Called	Touchdown %
1	100%	0	0%

Cover 1		Cover 2		Cover 0	
Called	Average	Called	Average	Called	Average
3	2.3	5.0	9.0	0.0	0.0

Cover 3		Cover 4	
Called	Average	Called	Average
6	9.5	3	-0.3

Cover 5		Drop 8	
Called	Average	Called	Average
2	15.5	1	0.0

Week	Quarter	Time	Down	ToGo	Location	Yards
Week 6 vs LA	2	1:29	1	10	SFO 50	0
Week 7 vs WAS	2	11:44	2	12	WAS 21	0
Week 7 vs WAS	2	0:53	1	10	WAS 49	0
Week 7 vs WAS	4	5:15	3	4	SFO 39	16
Week 10 vs SEA	1	13:45	3	10	SFO 25	16
Week 10 vs SEA	1	12:19	1	10	SEA 49	0
Week 10 vs SEA	2	14:20	3	8	SFO 28	5
Week 10 vs SEA	2	10:11	1	10	SFO 27	0
Week 10 vs SEA	3	10:12	3	11	SEA 42	9
Week 11 vs ARI	2	15:00	3	9	SFO 16	-9
Week 11 vs ARI	4	1:27	2	3	CRD 40	5
Week 13 vs BAL	1	6:37	3	6	SFO 31	-8
Week 14 vs NO	2	2:57	3	10	SFO 20	20
Week 15 vs ATL	4	2:09	2	8	ATL 32	4
Week 16 vs LAR	2	5:43	3	10	SFO 38	12
Week 16 vs LAR	4	6:14	3	7	RAM 7	7
Week 17 vs SEA	2	7:42	1	15	SEA 41	26
Week 17 vs SEA	3	13:38	3	15	SFO 20	7
SB vs KC	3	3:58	3	8	KAN 37	26
SB vs KC	4	9:47	3	14	SFO 34	3

Progression
1. Alert: Single Receiver Fade/Comeback/Corner
2. Inside Dig
3. Outside Dig
4. Return / Check Down

This concept was very multiple for the 49ers in 2019. With

the ability to use virtually any protection with it, and its adaptability to coverages, I consider it an all-purpose component of their drop back pass game.

The 7th and 8th diagrams show the "4 man" variation. I will use this term to refer to this specific way of running the concept for the rest of the section.

Against 2 high safeties, this play will high/low the strong hook defender. The "4 man" variation bumps this read to the middle linebacker. The images below shows these two drawn up.

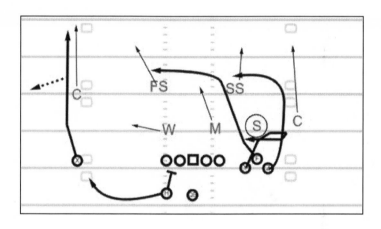

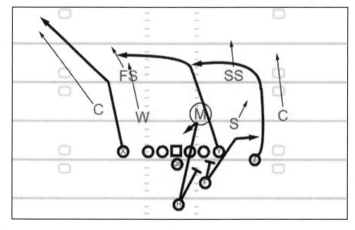

Against a single high safety, the stretch on the weak side of the formation will have a better chance of opening up. If the weak hook player turns and walls the first dig, the offense should still have inside leverage on the return route with the flat defender, and getting the high/low on the strong hook player. The two conflict defenders are circled in the following diagram, and the three options for the QB are shown with triangles. It's a 3 on 2 in favor of the offense. The "4 man" variation gets the high/low on the strong hook player, regardless. The images below show the concept.

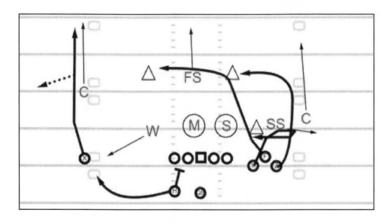

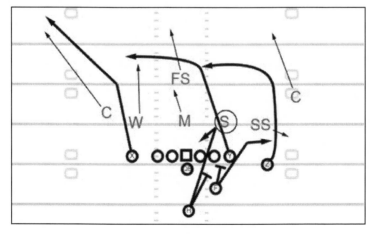

The "4 man" variation allows for the offense to max protect against a blitz if need be. Either dig route serves as a good route to get open vs true man coverage as well.

Against "lock & level" (true man) and "point/traffic" bunch checks, the return route should open up nicely. Against point/traffic, the "1st inside" defender will have a hi-low with he outside dig and return. The return will have inside leverage on the "1st outside" defender the image below shows the play.

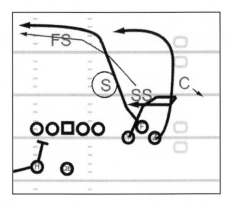

Why it Worked: This play makes great sense for third and mediums. The conversions in week 13 and week 7 show the concept working well against teams that man/zone match the vertical stems of the dig routes. Accurate throws on the inside dig also allow for big run after the catch opportunities. A nice window opens up against Seattle's cover 2 in week 17.

Why it Didn't Work: In week 13, the Ravens played a "box" check to the bunch side. This check gives the defense 4 over 3, creating a zone-match "box" around the bunch. The image below shows the initial alignment.

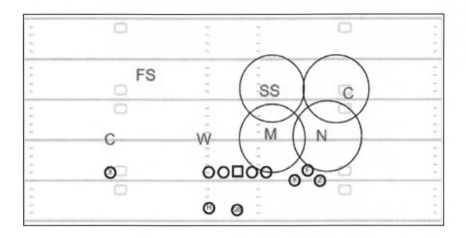

With this particular concept, the Ravens have good leverage on all of the routes, with he possible exception of the outside dig on the corner. With the free safety not playing the deep half, Garoppolo peaks the singled up receiver on the fade. By the time he gets back to the digs side, the creative fire zone pressure gets home for the Ravens.

In 3rd and long situations, defenses can play traditional zone coverages and match the digs with depth. When the quarterback takes an underneath route, rally and make the tackle short of the sticks.

Poor spacing from the outside dig and return route forces a contested throw on 2nd down in week 7. This play corresponds to the 3rd diagram. A tighter split on the outside dig would allow the route to hit the window before the return route, instead of at the same time.

On the first 3rd down in week 6, the mighty Aaron Donald gets home and does not allow Garoppolo to work the outside dig – return combo.

Flood

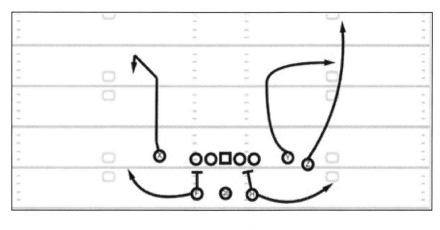

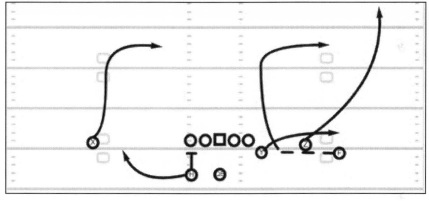

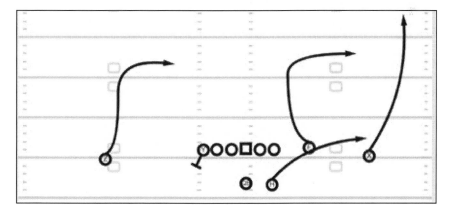

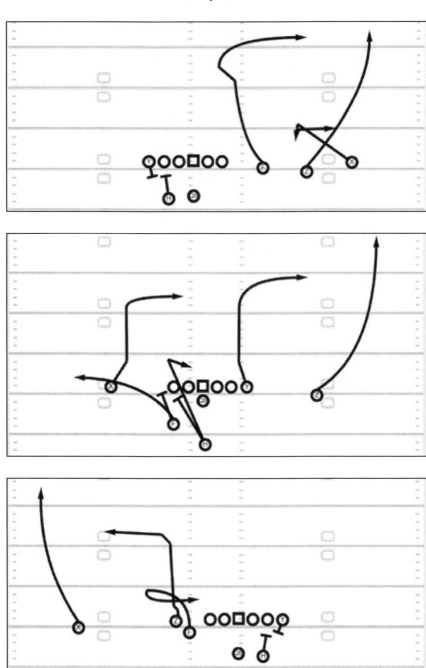

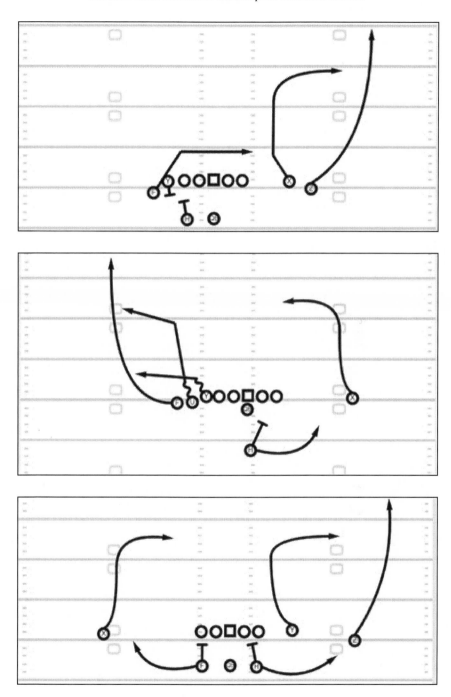

Average Yards per Play	2.9

1st Down		3rd/4th Down (includes RZ)	
Called	Average	Called	Success Rate
3	-3.0	5	50%
2nd Down 6-1		2nd Down 7+	
Called	Average	Called	Average
1	0.0	6	-0.8
Red Zone 10-0		Red Zone 10-20	
Called	Touchdown %	Called	Touchdown %
0	0%	1	0%

Cover 1		Cover 2		Cover 0	
Called	Average	Called	Average	Called	Average
3	3.3	1.0	-9.0	0.0	0.0
Cover 3		Cover 4			
Called	Average	Called	Average		
5	8.0	3	0.0		
Cover 5		Drop 8			
Called	Average	Called	Average		
0	0.0	1	0.0		

Week	Quarter	Time	Down	ToGo	Location	Yards
Week 2 vs CIN	2	4:54	3	12	CIN 39	0
Week 5 vs CLE	2	0:25	2	13	CLE 41	7
Week 6 vs LA	2	0:12	1	10	RAM 37	0
Week 6 vs LA	2	0:08	2	10	RAM 37	0
Week 7 vs WAS	2	0:58	2	9	SFO 46	0
Week 8 vs CAR	3	12:48	2	7	SFO 5	-5
Week 9 vs ARI	3	7:47	3	4	CRD 46	22
Week 11 vs ARI	3	5:32	3	5	CRD 12	TO
Week 12 vs GB	2	0:08	2	10	GNB 30	0
Week 13 vs BAL	1	12:00	4	2	RAV 33	33
Week 13 vs BAL	1	5:20	2	4	SFO 36	0
Week 14 vs NO	4	4:28	1	10	SFO 35	0
Week 16 vs LAR	4	1:04	2	9	SFO 38	-7
DIV vs MIN	1	1:18	1	10	MIN 36	-9
DIV vs MIN	1	0:30	3	24	SFO 50	0

This section focuses on the flood variations that are not used with play action. Without play action, a backside dig combination is typically used.

The second diagram shows a version that gets the intermediate route a free release with motion.

The third diagram shows a variation used into the boundary for end of half/end of game scenarios.

The 9th diagram shows a version where the 49ers can get 7 man protection, or bump the edge rushers to help the tackles in pass protection. This element allows the intermediate out cut to work further down field and buy the QB more time.

Why it Worked: The 6th diagram shows a variation with a return route used out of a condensed set. This version opened up nicely in week 9 and week 14. In week 13 they get a jump ball to Samuel down the sideline for a touchdown.

Why it Didn't Work: In Week 16, the receivers could not get off the jam, and pressure got to Garoppolo quickly.

Shallow

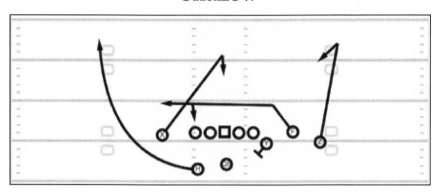

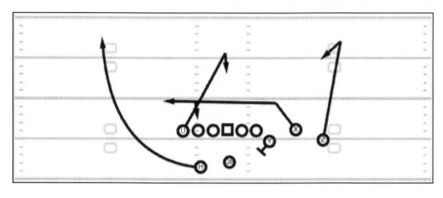

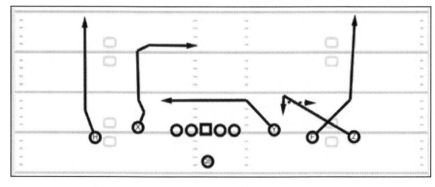

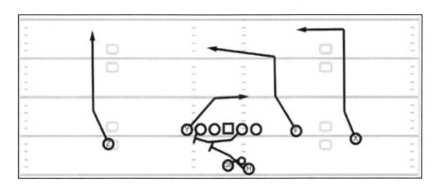

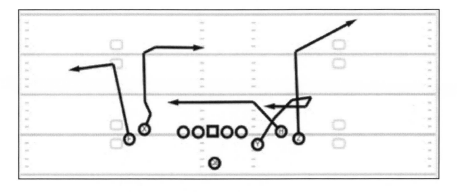

Average Yards per Play	3.0

1st Down		3rd/4th Down (includes RZ)	
Called	Average	Called	Success Rate
0	0.0	5	60%
2nd Down 6-1		**2nd Down 7+**	
Called	Average	Called	Average
1	-6.0	1	8.0
Red Zone 10-0		**Red Zone 10-20**	
Called	Touchdown %	Called	Touchdown %
0	0%	1	0%

Cover 1		Cover 2		Cover 0	
Called	Average	Called	Average	Called	Average
4	2.3	2.0	2.0	0.0	0.0

Cover 3		Cover 4	
Called	Average	Called	Average
1	8.0	0	0.0

Cover 5		Drop 8	
Called	Average	Called	Average
0	0.0	1	0.0

Week	Quarter	Time	Down	ToGo	Location	Yards
Week 2 vs CIN	2	0:44	3	5	CIN 35	7
Week 6 vs LA	1	6:54	3	3	SFO 43	10
Week 6 vs LA	4	8:49	3	5	RAM 40	-2
Week 8 vs CAR	2	2:28	3	4	SFO 43	4
Week 12 vs GB	2	3:30	2	10	GNB 17	8
Week 15 vs ATL	3	12:53	3	5	SFO 48	0
Week 17 vs SEA	1	13:07	2	6	SFO 25	-6

Progression Read:
1. HB Rail/Fade/Comeback
2. Shallow
3. Dig/Search Route

While the shallow cross package is not a big part of Kyle Shanahan's offense, it has a place in his third down package.

The first diagram shows the most commonly used variation, especially earlier in the season. This version is a good example of Shanahan mixing up his protections. He keeps the tight end in to block, and free releases the running back. This protection is a nice adjustment for teams that like to "blitz the back", which means they base their blitz off which side the running back is lined up on.

The fourth diagram shows a pop pass variation that was used in week 12.

The fifth diagram shows a similar concept to the third diagram, but instead the two man combination is the smash-return concept. This version as used in week 15.

Why it Worked: In week 2, the shallow breaks free from man coverage. In 1Q week 6, the Rams do a nice job of taking away the shallow in their 1-robber coverage, but Jimmy Garoppolo does a nice job of climbing the pocket to get to his third read. He hits Kittle on the search route for a nice first down. .In week 8, Garoppolo gets to his fourth read diagram 3 version, the snag route.

Why it Didn't Work: in 4Q week 6, Garoppolo's first three options are covered nicely, and the pressure gets to him before he can scramble. In week 15, the Falcons cover it up by dropping 8 into coverage. The underneath defenders play with proper leverage and take away the return route from Kittle.

Mesh

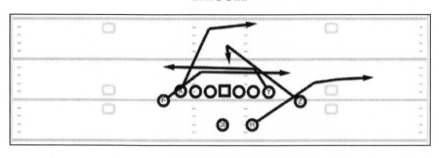

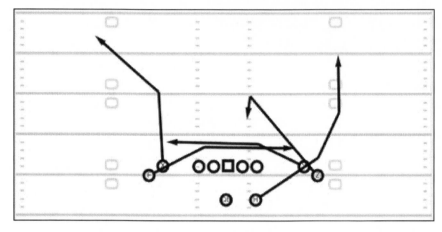

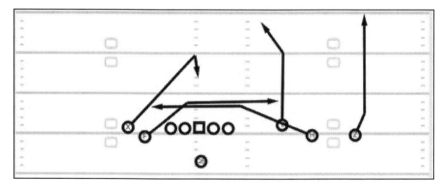

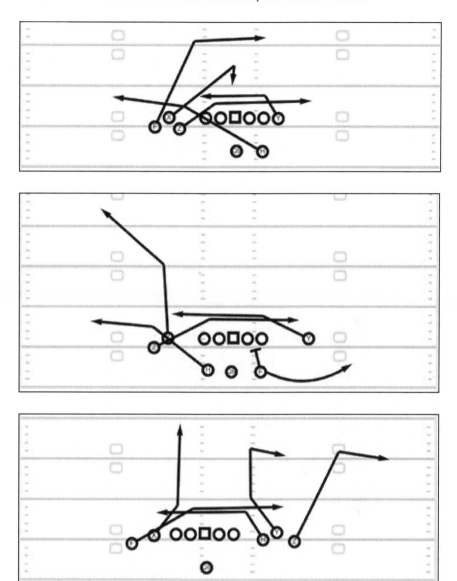

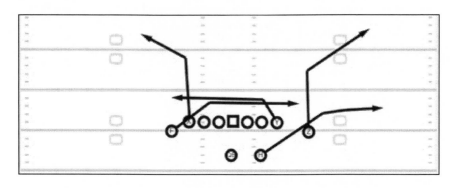

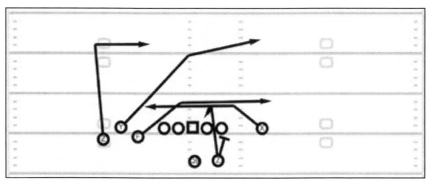

Average Yards per Play	12.2

1st Down		3rd/4th Down (includes RZ)	
Called	Average	Called	Success Rate
3	19.3	5	40%
2nd Down 6-1		**2nd Down 7+**	
Called	Average	Called	Average
1	5.0	0	0.0
Red Zone 10-0		**Red Zone 10-20**	
Called	Touchdown %	Called	Touchdown %
3	33%	0	0%

Cover 1		Cover 2		Cover 0	
Called	Average	Called	Average	Called	Average
3	15.0	0.0	0.0	3.0	2.3

Cover 3		Cover 4	
Called	Average	Called	Average
3	19.3	0	0.0

Cover 5		Drop 8	
Called	Average	Called	Average
0	0.0	0	0.0

Week	Quarter	Time	Down	ToGo	Location	Yards
Week 6 vs LA	3	5:06	3	2	RAM 2	0
Week 7 vs WAS	1	3:59	3	7	SFO 42	0
Week 11 vs ARI	3	14:52	1	10	SFO 16	37
Week 11 vs ARI	3	11:11	2	5	CRD 5	5
Week 11 vs ARI	3	1:30	3	9	SFO 26	26
Week 15 vs ATL	2	6:27	3	5	SFO 30	0
Week 16 vs LAR	4	7:02	1	9	RAM 9	2
DIV vs MIN	3	14:32	3	5	SFO 42	21
NFCCG vs GB	4	8:10	1	10	SFO 27	19

Progression Read: Changes based on which variation is used.

Mesh is a great way to create man coverage rubs within the framework of a pass concept. Mesh is best when paired with zone beating routes as the first part of the progression.

Diagrams 1 and 4 were used in the low red zone. The fourth diagram shows the touchdown from week 11.

Why it Worked: In week 11, Garoppolo makes a great throw under pressure on the corner route. Not to mention, the incredible catch from Samuel on that play as well.

The 37 yard gainer in week 11 was the result of a zone defender not staying with one of the underneath crossing routes. The corner on that side collapsed inside with the search route over the ball, leaving no help up the sideline. This version can be seen in the third diagram.

Why it Didn't Work: In week 7, Washington did a great job of passing the routes off within their man coverage scheme (Cover 1 Rat). In week 15, the Falcons were able to generate quick pressure on Garoppolo with a simulated pressure and force a bad throw.

PA Naked – Slide Delay

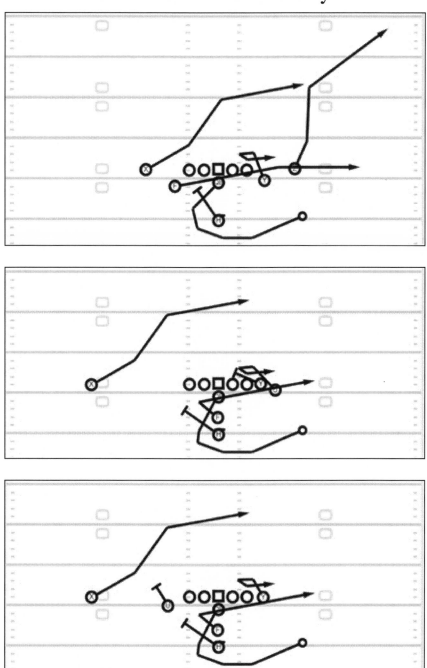

Bobby Peters

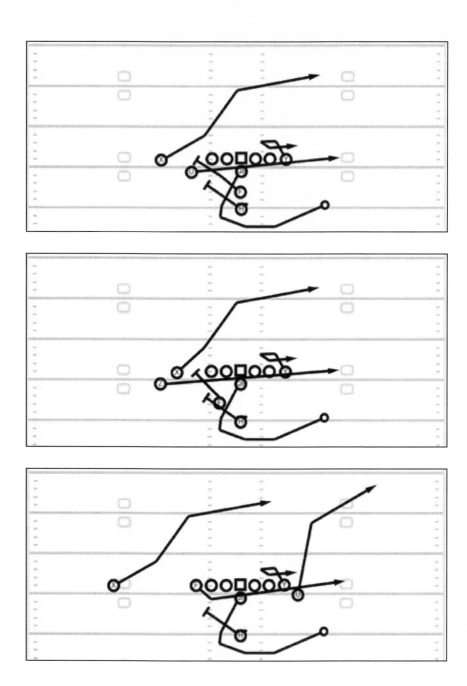

272

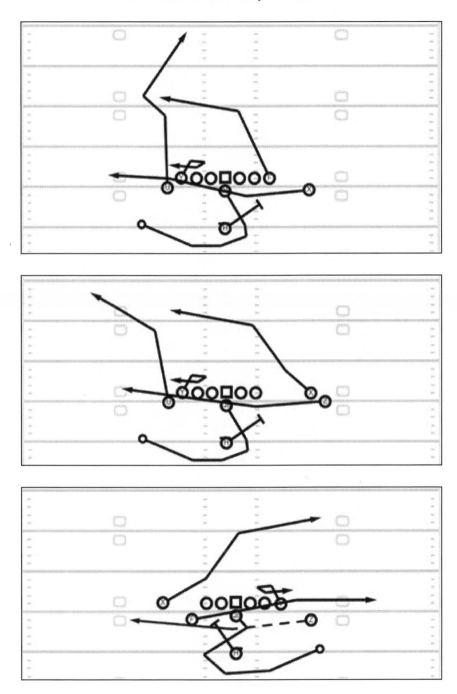

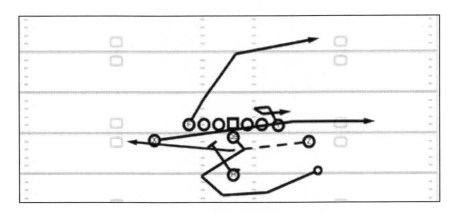

Average Yards per Play	11.0

1st Down		3rd/4th Down (includes RZ)	
Called	Average	Called	Success Rate
10	14.0	1	0%
2nd Down 6-1		**2nd Down 7+**	
Called	Average	Called	Average
4	7.3	1	7.0
Red Zone 10-0		**Red Zone 10-20**	
Called	Touchdown %	Called	Touchdown %
2	50%	3	0%

Cover 1		Cover 2		Cover 0	
Called	Average	Called	Average	Called	Average
5	4.8	1.0	16.0	1.0	0.0
Cover 3		**Cover 4**			
Called	Average	Called	Average		
8	9.4	1	61.0		
Cover 5		**Drop 8**			
Called	Average	Called	Average		
0	0.0	0	0.0		

Week	Quarter	Time	Down	ToGo	Location	Yards
Week 2 vs CIN	2	11:02	1	10	CIN 15	9
Week 2 vs CIN	2	5:43	2	9	CIN 36	7
Week 7 vs WAS	1	0:29	1	10	WAS 40	0
Week 7 vs WAS	3	8:10	1	10	WAS 30	15
Week 7 vs WAS	4	10:23	2	4	WAS 4	2
Week 10 vs SEA	4	8:18	2	2	SEA 33	10
Week 12 vs GB	3	3:05	1	10	SFO 39	61
Week 14 vs NO	3	10:28	1	10	NOR 20	15
Week 14 vs NO	3	9:46	1	5	NOR 5	5
Week 15 vs ATL	1	8:22	2	6	SFO 16	5
Week 15 vs ATL	4	3:44	1	10	SFO 37	0
Week 16 vs LAR	2	6:24	1	10	SFO 38	0
Week 17 vs SEA	1	10:36	2	2	SFO 43	12
Week 17 vs SEA	2	11:27	1	10	SFO 17	19
DIV vs MIN	3	10:54	3	2	MIN 17	0
NFCCG vs GB	1	9:33	1	10	SFO 11	16

Play action bootlegs are common at every level of football. This concept is a great compliment to a zone running system.

The play can be read many ways. This variation is typically taught like this:

Progression Read:

1. Corner Route
2. Slide Route
3. 10-15 yard crossing route
4. Delay route.

This variation is my personal favorite. This one gives the quarterback three immediate layers on his front side, with the delay route working late after sealing the edge for him. Due to formation and motioning, not every variation has the corner route.

The 7th diagram shows a variation used in week 12 for a big touchdown. The play appears to be a "can" when the offense sees quarters coverage pre-snap.

Why it Worked: The clip from the NFCCG gets Samuel on the slide route, and gives Garoppolo an easy completion early in the game.

On back to back plays in week 14, Garoppolo hits the slide route to get into the end zone. The touchdown clip brings the slide route from the in line tight end position (6th diagram).

Why it Didn't Work: Without a front side corner route, the defense has a better chance of covering up the concept. In week 15, the front side corner in a cover 3 scheme is able to help on the deep crossing route without a vertical threat.

In week 16, the edge rusher pays no attention to protecting his backside run game and gets upfield to rush Garoppolo into a bad throw.

PA Naked – Drive

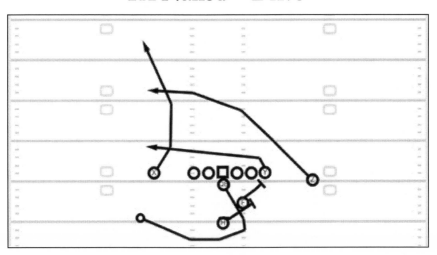

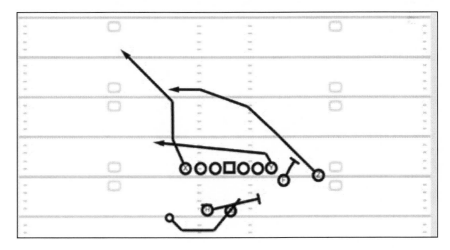

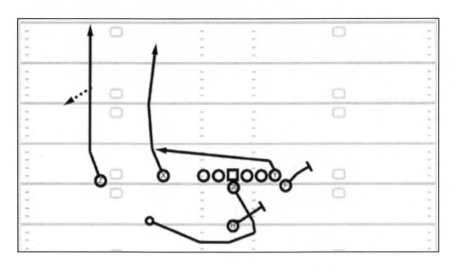

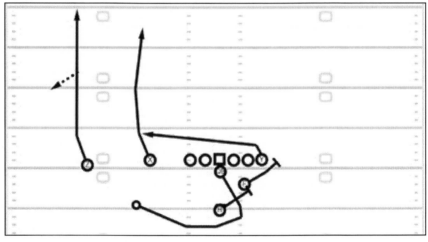

Average Yards per Play	7.0

1st Down		3rd/4th Down (includes RZ)	
Called	Average	Called	Success Rate
4	8.0	0	0%
2nd Down 6-1		2nd Down 7+	
Called	Average	Called	Average
1	4.0	3	6.7
Red Zone 10-0		Red Zone 10-20	
Called	Touchdown %	Called	Touchdown %
0	0%	0	0%

Cover 1		Cover 2		Cover 0	
Called	Average	Called	Average	Called	Average
1	0.0	1.0	4.0	0.0	0.0
Cover 3		Cover 4			
Called	Average	Called	Average		
5	6.6	1	19.0		
Cover 5		Drop 8			
Called	Average	Called	Average		
0	0.0	0	0.0		

Week	Quarter	Time	Down	ToGo	Location	Yards
Week 1 vs TB	1	13:08	2	9	TAM 32	19
Week 1 vs TB	3	14:29	2	8	SFO 27	0
Week 2 vs CIN	1	5:23	2	7	SFO 33	1
Week 5 vs CLE	2	4:45	1	10	CLE 49	13
Week 7 vs WAS	3	14:01	1	10	WAS 44	0
Week 9 vs ARI	3	13:21	1	10	SFO 41	0
Week 13 vs BAL	3	8:54	2	5	RAV 43	4
Week 14 vs NO	1	11:34	1	10	SFO 25	19

In this variation, the underneath route will work behind the defensive line. With an in-line tight end, this is how the 49ers would typically get him on the underneath route. Although they would fake the slice block occasionally from this alignment, they primarily used him on the drive route.

The 49ers often combined their naked action with tempo. Combining nakeds with tempo is something that Shanahan has done for years. Using tempo will typically get the 2nd level defenders to flow faster to their run keys if they are late to the ball being snapped out of panic. This was the case in week 1.

Why it Worked: In week 5, the drive route works across the seam/flat defenders face.

In week 14, Garoppolo hits the fall out comeback on the front side on the first play of the game.

Why it Didn't Work: In week 7, the corner matches the drive route from depth and follows him with good leverage across the field.

In week 9, the Cardinals cut the drive with a "rat" call in a cover 1 coverage. The corner carries the deep crossing route tightly as well

PA Naked – Others

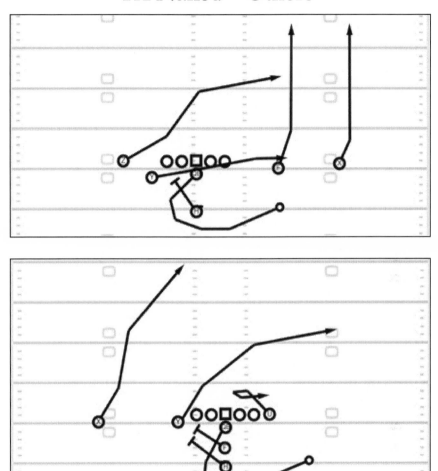

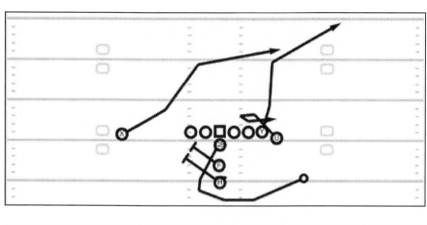

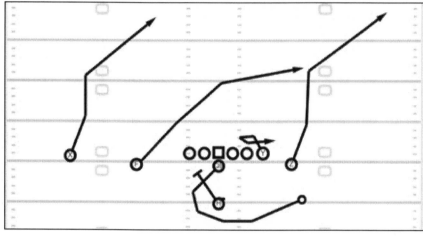

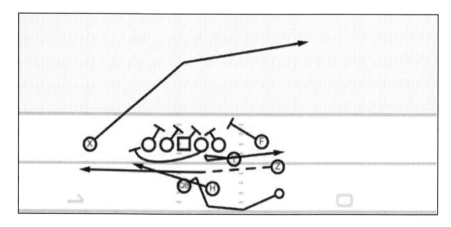

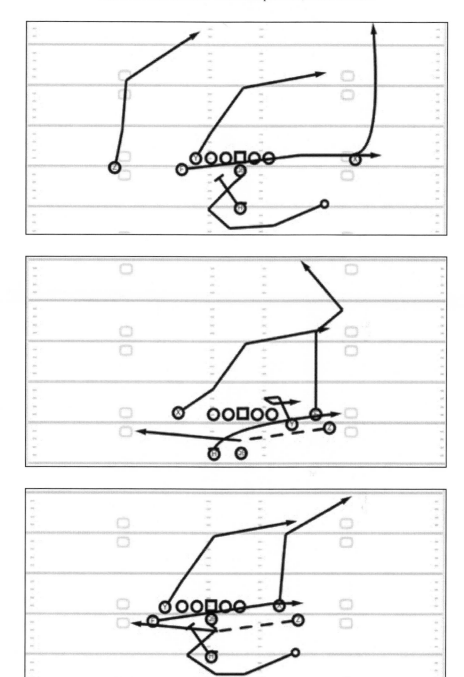

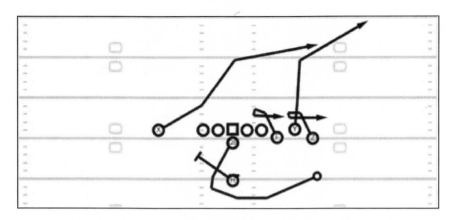

Average Yards per Play	14.5

1st Down		3rd/4th Down (includes RZ)	
Called	Average	Called	Success Rate
14	17.4	0	0%
2nd Down 6-1		**2nd Down 7+**	
Called	Average	Called	Average
3	0.0	3	15.3
Red Zone 10-0		**Red Zone 10-20**	
Called	Touchdown %	Called	Touchdown %
1	0%	3	33%

Cover 1		Cover 2		Cover 0	
Called	Average	Called	Average	Called	Average
6	13.0	2.0	45.0	4.0	6.3
Cover 3		**Cover 4**			
Called	Average	Called	Average		
5	13.2	3	10.0		
Cover 5		**Drop 8**			
Called	Average	Called	Average		
0	0.0	0	0.0		

Week	Quarter	Time	Down	ToGo	Location	Yards
Week 1 vs TB	3	3:29	1	10	TAM 39	0
Week 1 vs TB	4	12:27	2	7	SFO 5	6
Week 2 vs CIN	3	3:09	1	10	SFO 18	36
Week 3 vs PIT	2	9:15	2	6	PIT 22	0
Week 6 vs LA	3	5:13	2	2	RAM 2	0
Week 9 vs ARI	2	10:46	1	10	CRD 23	12
Week 11 vs ARI	1	10:31	1	10	SFO 25	4
Week 12 vs GB	3	3:52	1	10	SFO 25	14
Week 14 vs NO	2	14:57	1	10	SFO 25	75
Week 14 vs NO	2	4:16	1	10	SFO 20	7
Week 14 vs NO	4	11:47	1	10	NOR 37	0
Week 15 vs ATL	3	2:37	1	10	SFO 27	21
Week 15 vs ATL	4	3:37	2	10	SFO 37	29
Week 17 vs SEA	1	1:44	1	10	SFO 49	15
Week 17 vs SEA	4	8:37	1	10	SFO 45	16
DIV vs MIN	2	8:19	1	10	MIN 19	18
NFCCG vs GB	1	0:45	2	6	GNB 28	0
SB vs KC	1	13:18	2	11	SFO 17	11
SB vs KC	2	5:13	1	10	KAN 15	15
SB vs KC	3	3:21	1	10	KAN 11	10

This section comprises of the variations that don't fit into the previous categories.

The first diagram shows the variation used in week 12. Against single high coverage, the two verticals get carried and leaves the hook defender to the naked side in a 2 on 1.

The 5th diagram shows a red zone variation used off of a fake shovel pass action.

The last diagram shows the version the 49ers called three times in the Super Bowl.

Why it Worked: In week 2, Kittle works free on the crossing route vs man coverage. In week 14, Garoppolo takes a shot on the Cop route for a big gain.

Similar to the other versions, this concept is a sound way to compliment a strong running game. The pocket movement is a great way to buy time for the quarterback, and the route combinations flood his vision on the front side of the play.

Jimmy Garoppolo excelled at throwing off platform, and this concept is a great illustration. Plenty of production on this concept came from him rolling to his left with pressure coming down on him.

Why it Didn't Work: In week 1, Garoppolo throws the ball behind the receiver on the crossing route (still catchable, however).

PA Bang Dig/Post/Slant

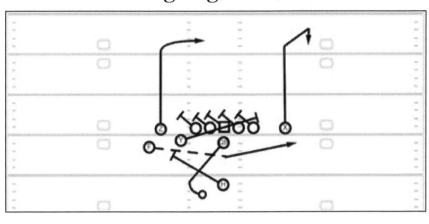

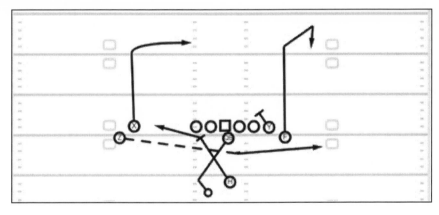

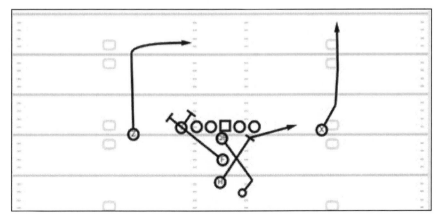

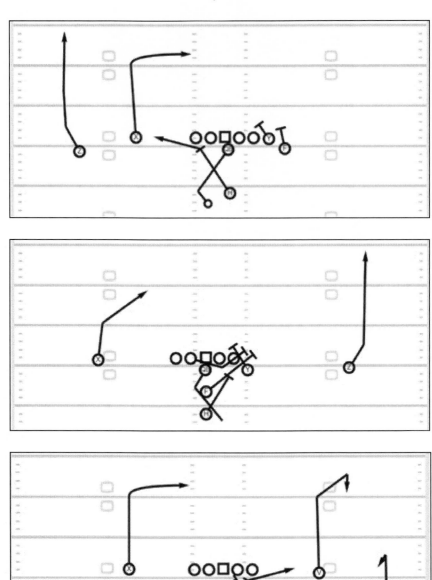

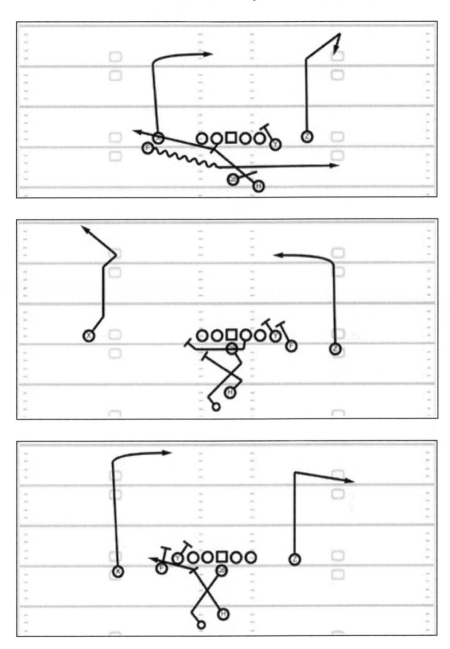

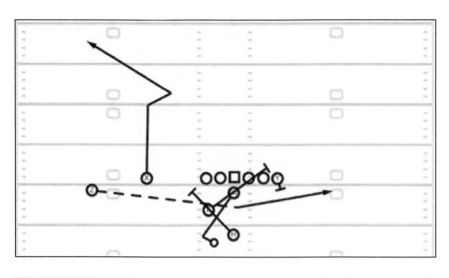

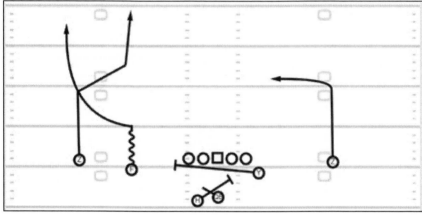

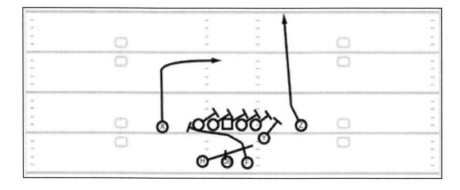

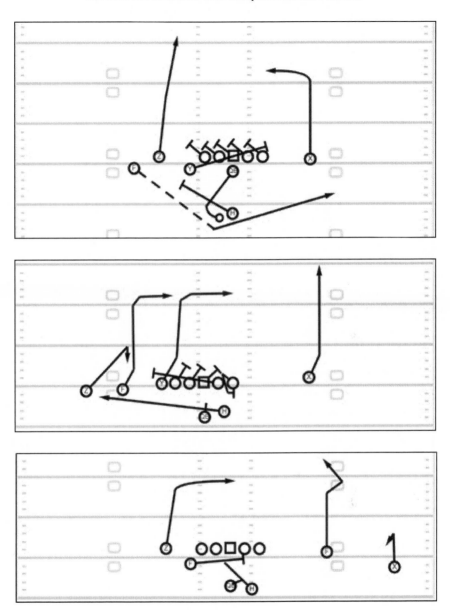

Average Yards per Play	10.8

1st Down		3rd/4th Down (includes RZ)	
Called	Average	Called	Success Rate
13	9.5	0	0%
2nd Down 6-1		2nd Down 7+	
Called	Average	Called	Average
4	10.5	8	13.6
Red Zone 10-0		Red Zone 10-20	
Called	Touchdown %	Called	Touchdown %
2	50%	0	0%

Cover 1		Cover 2		Cover 0	
Called	Average	Called	Average	Called	Average
4	4.8	0.0	0.0	2.0	1.5
Cover 3		Cover 4			
Called	Average	Called	Average		
18	13.1	1	16.0		
Cover 5		Drop 8			
Called	Average	Called	Average		
0	0.0	0	0.0		

Week	Quarter	Time	Down	ToGo	Location	Yards
Week 1 vs TB	3	12:38	2	9	TAM 39	39
Week 1 vs TB	4	4:47	1	10	SFO 25	0
Week 2 vs CIN	1	6:35	2	10	SFO 16	14
Week 3 vs PIT	1	4:52	2	11	SFO 27	TO
Week 3 vs PIT	2	12:29	1	10	PIT 40	16
Week 3 vs PIT	4	7:00	2	7	PIT 7	0
Week 5 vs CLE	3	11:59	1	10	CLE 37	14
Week 5 vs CLE	4	10:27	1	10	SFO 16	10
Week 6 vs LA	1	1:35	1	10	SFO 24	14
Week 6 vs LA	4	6:46	2	10	SFO 28	0
Week 8 vs CAR	1	11:54	1	10	CAR 41	0
Week 8 vs CAR	2	9:39	1	10	SFO 33	12
Week 9 vs ARI	2	4:00	1	10	CRD 44	4
Week 10 vs SEA	1	4:23	2	8	SEA 24	12
Week 12 vs GB	1	10:46	2	2	SFO 46	15
Week 14 vs NO	1	10:32	1	15	SFO 39	31
Week 15 vs ATL	1	4:26	1	10	ATL 45	0
Week 15 vs ATL	2	6:32	2	5	SFO 30	0
Week 15 vs ATL	3	14:14	1	10	SFO 43	3
Week 17 vs SEA	1	2:20	2	7	SFO 19	30
DIV vs MIN	1	9:33	1	3	MIN 3	3
SB vs KC	3	14:18	2	5	SFO 21	15
SB vs KC	3	5:23	1	10	SFO 45	16
SB vs KC	4	11:18	2	4	SFO 26	12
SB vs KC	4	9:52	2	9	SFO 39	0

The bang dig off of play action is one of Shanahan's staple concepts, and is incredibly efficient for him every year.

It seemed like each week the 49ers had a new way to run the concept. Being multiple with this particular scheme does not put too much extra stress on the offense, while not allowing the defense to pick up any formation/motion tendencies.

The bang dig is the primary target on this concept. The only real exception is the 11th diagram. In this version, the 49ers are trying to hit the "stalk rail" route for a big play.

The mini-dig route has the receiver make his cut on his

fifth or seventh step. The angle of the route varies based on how the defense is structured and the split of the receiver.

The concept is so effective because the 49ers see so much single high coverage on early run downs. In fact, the 49ers never saw two high safeties with this play called. They could very well "Can It" (audible) vs two high safeties into a run play as well.

The linebackers have to fit their run gaps, the free safety has to get depth, and the corners have to play outside with their proper divider leverage in match coverage. This leaves a huge void over the middle.

Defenses that base out of a cover 4 would give this scheme trouble. The robbing safety is in great position to take the route away.

For high school and college coaches, this play is an easy addition to your current playbook. Marry it off of your base run action, and your quarterback will have an opportunity for an easy completion down the field.

The fourteenth diagram shows a variation with two dig routes coming from the same side. The 49ers formation trey into the boundary and fake their trap scheme with it.

Why it Worked: The "stalk rail" route hit for a big play in week 1. The 3 step slant variation opened up in week 10 and week 17. In general, the scheme is sound and Garoppolo's quick release and timing made for some big plays.

Why it Didn't Work: In week 15, the Falcons show how

corners can leverage the route in a single high structure. One of the clips shows a version of cover 3 with a safety playing the weak hook from depth. Garoppolo wisely holds on to the ball here instead of trying to force it in.

In week 3, Pettis rounds his route which allows the corner to make a play on the ball. The corner also had a nice beat on the route too. Additionally, the protection breaks down. The 49ers fake their counter scheme, and the Steelers bring heat off the edge. With the tackle blocking down hard, the DE squeezes hard because he has to cross the tackles face to get to the B gap. The pulling guard does not see him because he is so tight to the tackle, attempting to get inside (which he is unable to do) The pulling guard instead goes for the player off the edge. The running back is responsible for the edge pressure here. The play is shown below.

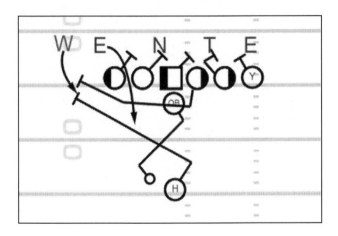

PA Leak

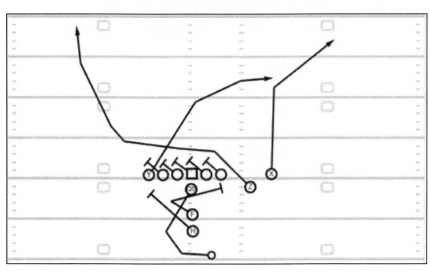

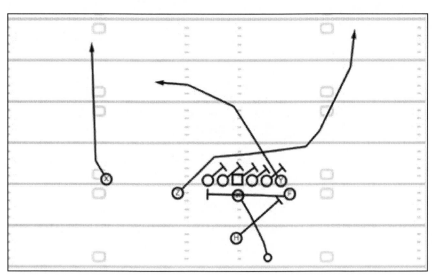

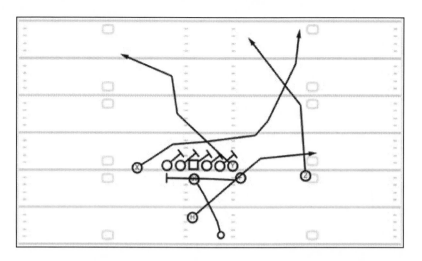

Average Yards per Play	15.8

1st Down		3rd/4th Down (includes RZ)	
Called	Average	Called	Success Rate
5	15.8	0	0%
2nd Down 6-1		**2nd Down 7+**	
Called	Average	Called	Average
0	0.0	0	0.0
Red Zone 10-0		**Red Zone 10-20**	
Called	Touchdown %	Called	Touchdown %
0	0%	0	0%

Cover 1		Cover 2		Cover 0	
Called	Average	Called	Average	Called	Average
3	20.0	0.0	0.0	0.0	0.0
Cover 3		**Cover 4**			
Called	Average	Called	Average		
2	9.5	0	0.0		
Cover 5		**Drop 8**			
Called	Average	Called	Average		
0	0.0	0	0.0		

Week	Quarter	Time	Down	ToGo	Location	Yards
Week 2 vs CIN	1	11:21	1	10	CIN 38	38
Week 7 vs WAS	4	11:44	1	10	WAS 33	26
Week 11 vs ARI	3	2:54	1	10	SFO 25	-7
Week 12 vs GB	2	5:33	1	10	SFO 50	22
Week 14 vs NO	3	4:51	1	10	SFO 25	0

The "Leak concept is a Kyle Shanahan staple that seems to be infiltrating every playbook around the NFL. The play is a misdirection shot play designed to constraint their bootleg play action game. The "leak" route can be roughly described as a wheel route coming from the other side of the field. With the route coming from the other side of the field, it is easy to get lost vs the many match coverages prevalent in football. In man coverage, the initial path looks like a hard down block. The man defender has a lot of traffic to fight through as well.

The first diagram shows the play from week 2.

The last diagram shows the variation used in week 14.

Why it Worked: In week 2, the play hits big against cover 3. The corner on the side of the leak route takes the vertical stem of the #1 receiver, with everybody else playing run/naked.

Why it Didn't Work: The Cardinals leave the corner over the top in week 11. Pressure gets home in week 14.

PA Deep Hank/Curls

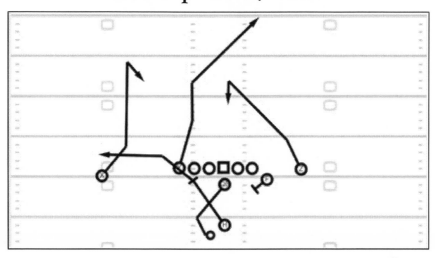

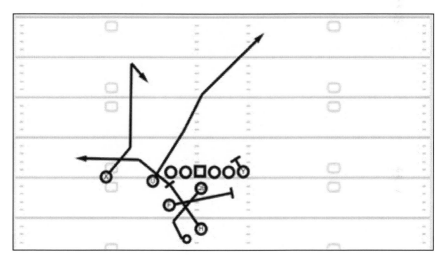

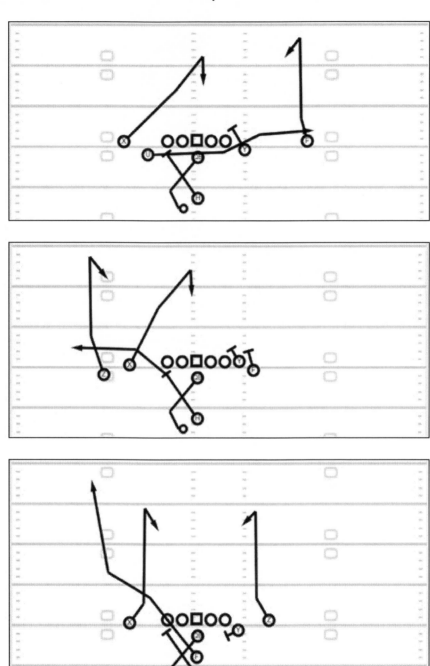

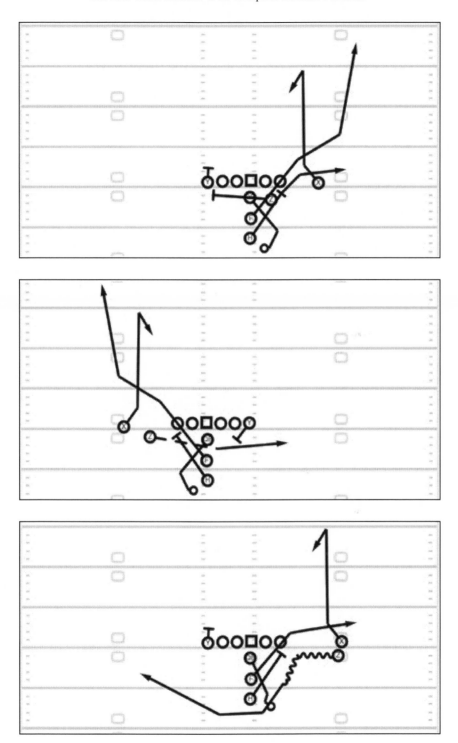

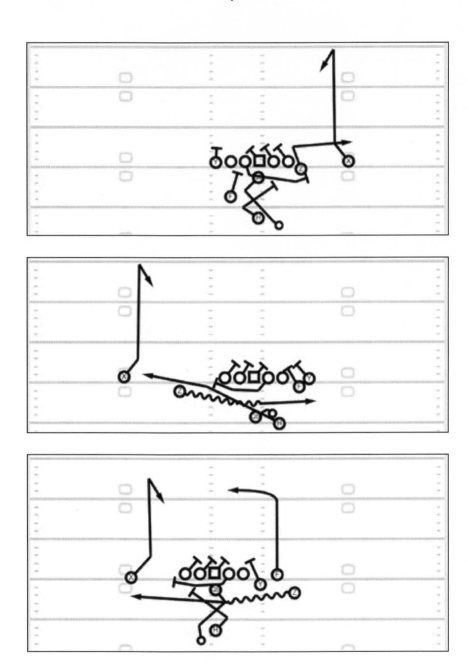

Average Yards per Play	10.3

1st Down		3rd/4th Down (includes RZ)	
Called	Average	Called	Success Rate
7	11.3	0	0%
2nd Down 6-1		**2nd Down 7+**	
Called	Average	Called	Average
5	11.0	1	0.0
Red Zone 10-0		**Red Zone 10-20**	
Called	Touchdown %	Called	Touchdown %
0	0%	1	0%

Cover 1		Cover 2		Cover 0	
Called	Average	Called	Average	Called	Average
4	9.5	0.0	0.0	0.0	0.0
Cover 3		**Cover 4**			
Called	Average	Called	Average		
9	10.7	0	0.0		
Cover 5		**Drop 8**			
Called	Average	Called	Average		
0	0.0	0	0.0		

Week	Quarter	Time	Down	ToGo	Location	Yards
Week 1 vs TB	2	1:25	1	10	TAM 19	-8
Week 3 vs PIT	1	0:55	1	10	SFO 45	27
Week 5 vs CLE	1	13:02	1	10	CLE 41	0
Week 5 vs CLE	3	13:21	2	6	SFO 34	17
Week 7 vs WAS	1	6:04	2	9	SFO 30	0
Week 9 vs ARI	2	12:28	1	10	SFO 24	20
Week 10 vs SEA	1	12:33	2	5	SFO 46	0
Week 10 vs SEA	4	9:42	2	6	SFO 35	24
Week 10 vs SEA	OT	4:58	2	6	SEA 45	0
Week 13 vs BAL	4	15:00	1	15	SFO 14	18
Week 15 vs ATL	4	5:15	1	10	SFO 25	4
SB vs KC	1	0:31	1	10	SFO 25	18
SB vs KC	3	12:36	2	6	KAN 46	14

With this concept being called on run downs vs single high coverages, the 49ers get the look they want. The curls will have inside leverage from condensed splits on the corner backs. The Inside defenders are occupied with the play fake.

A play caller is only limited by his creativity with this concept. The Deep Curl can be called off any run action.

If the corner backs start playing the curls aggressively, Shanahan will dial up the version with the fullback wheel route. This version as called in the Super Bowl, Week 3, 5, and 11.

Why it Worked: The fullback wheel route was the source of a big play in the Super Bowl and in week 3. The receivers ran sharp deep curl routes and Garoppolo had a good feel for the window on this throw.

Why it Didn't Work: Creative blitzes can give the play action protection issues. The overtime clip in week 10 is an example of how pressure can get the QB off his spot on this concept.

PA Flood

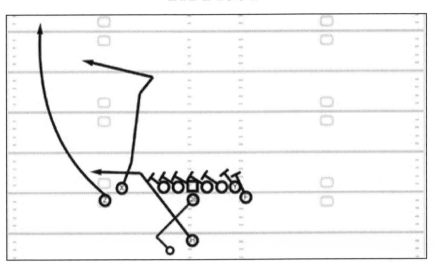

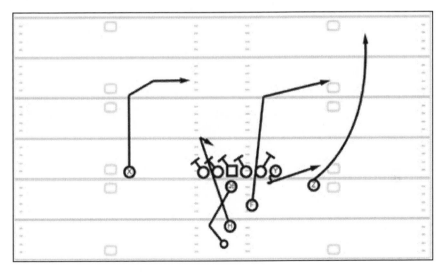

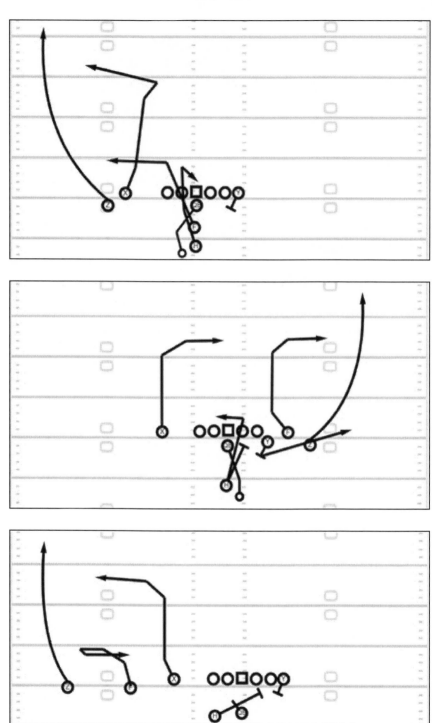

Average Yards per Play	24.5

1st Down		3rd/4th Down (includes RZ)	
Called	Average	Called	Success Rate
4	17.0	0	0%
2nd Down 6-1		**2nd Down 7+**	
Called	Average	Called	Average
1	25.0	3	29.3
Red Zone 10-0		**Red Zone 10-20**	
Called	Touchdown %	Called	Touchdown %
0	0%	0	0%

Cover 1		Cover 2		Cover 0	
Called	Average	Called	Average	Called	Average
3	17.5	0.0	0.0	0.0	0.0
Cover 3		**Cover 4**			
Called	Average	Called	Average		
4	22.3	1	45.0		
Cover 5		**Drop 8**			
Called	Average	Called	Average		
0	0.0	1	0.0		

Week	Quarter	Time	Down	ToGo	Location	Yards
Week 3 vs PIT	4	10:08	2	3	SFO 32	25
Week 6 vs LA	2	14:52	2	10	SFO 49	45
Week 7 vs WAS	3	14:23	2	7	SFO 28	28
Week 10 vs SEA	3	6:19	1	10	SFO 41	TO
Week 11 vs ARI	3	14:00	1	15	CRD 37	14
Week 15 vs ATL	2	2:00	1	10	ATL 43	20
Week 16 vs LAR	1	4:09	1	10	RAM 47	TO
Week 17 vs SEA	2	10:09	2	8	SFO 38	15

Play action flood concepts are a staple play action concept for many teams across all levels of football. What makes them so successful for the 49ers are the creative designs and strong execution.

Play action flood concepts are a great way to create easy reads for your quarterback. With the use of play action, you don't need to give him a backside progression. The play fake will hold the hook defenders, whereas in a true drop back setting the backside concept is needed incase the hook defenders flow to the flood side of the play.

The 2nd diagram shows one of my favorite designs from 2019. Getting the fullback (in this case it was Kittle lined up at fullback) on the intermediate route after an inside zone-lock-insert fake is a great way to get him free. With the Rams in a quarters coverage, the safety sees the tight end pass block, and goes to rob the #1 receiver. This leaves Kittle to run free in the second level after the linebacker bites on the run fake.

Off an inside release, the intermediate out route would often sell the crossing route at the top of the route. This stem and shake at the top created a lot for separation for the concept to work.

Why it Worked: Getting route runners like Kittle on an intermediate route vs man/match coverage off play action is a recipe for success. The protection held up, and Garoppolo usually delivered.

Why it Didn't Work: The Seattle interception was an high throw from Garoppolo that got tipped up to a safety by Bourne. The Rams interception was a great play from Ramsey to leave the return route and jump the deep out cut. This is a read Garoppolo could have picked up on, though.

PA Cross

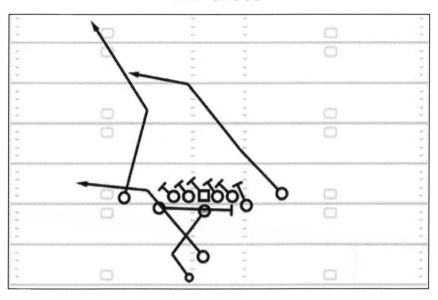

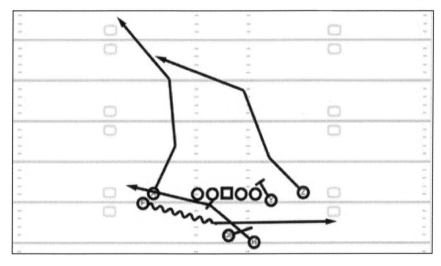

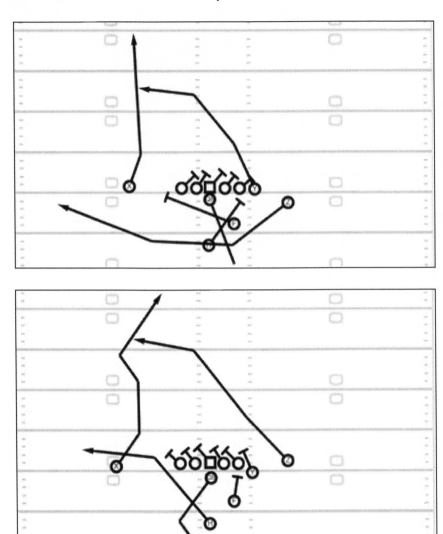

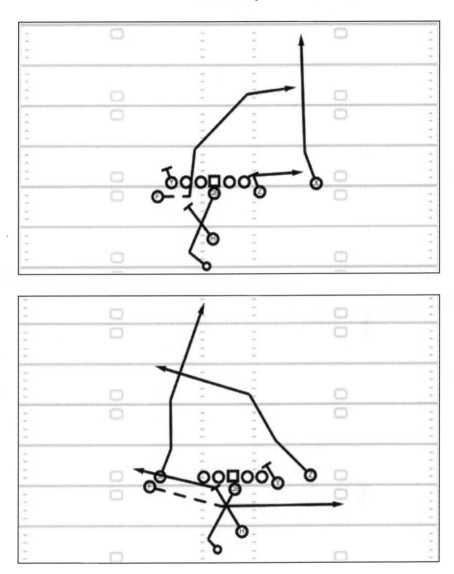

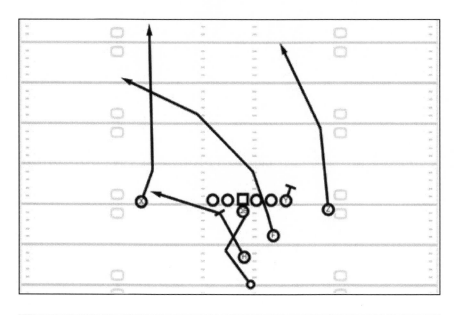

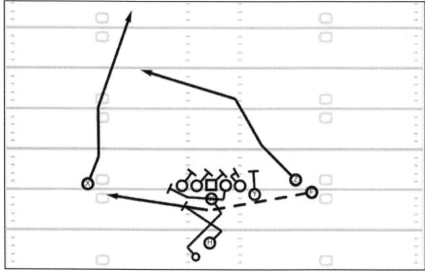

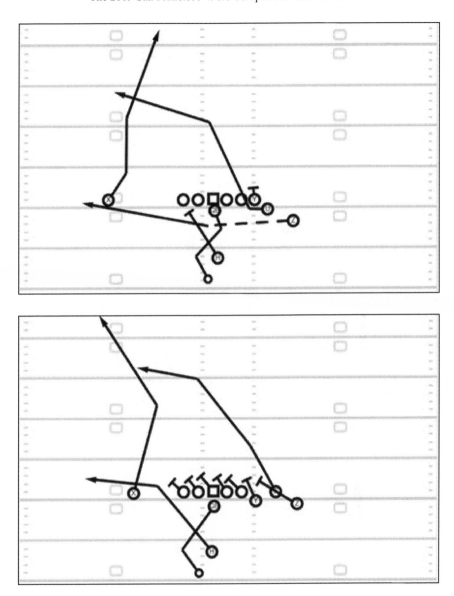

Average Yards per Play	10.3

1st Down		3rd/4th Down (includes RZ)	
Called	Average	Called	Success Rate
7	8.3	0	0%
2nd Down 6-1		**2nd Down 7+**	
Called	Average	Called	Average
1	12.0	5	12.8
Red Zone 10-0		**Red Zone 10-20**	
Called	Touchdown %	Called	Touchdown %
0	0%	0	0%

Cover 1		Cover 2		Cover 0	
Called	Average	Called	Average	Called	Average
1	0.0	3.0	5.7	0.0	0.0
Cover 3		**Cover 4**			
Called	Average	Called	Average		
8	14.6	1	9.0		
Cover 5		**Drop 8**			
Called	Average	Called	Average		
0	0.0	0	0.0		

Week	Quarter	Time	Down	ToGo	Location	Yards
Week 2 vs CIN	3	6:50	2	19	SFO 47	25
Week 3 vs PIT	1	14:29	2	5	SFO 30	12
Week 3 vs PIT	3	8:09	1	10	SFO 25	0
Week 5 vs CLE	2	11:22	1	10	SFO 25	0
Week 6 vs LA	3	10:33	2	9	SFO 44	8
Week 7 vs WAS	2	14:25	1	10	WAS 30	7
Week 7 vs WAS	2	2:35	2	10	SFO 42	0
Week 13 vs BAL	1	8:37	2	8	SFO 18	9
Week 14 vs NO	3	14:55	1	10	SFO 21	15
Week 15 vs ATL	2	2:36	1	15	SFO 20	0
Week 16 vs LAR	4	8:54	1	10	SFO 9	36
Week 17 vs SEA	2	9:33	1	10	SEA 47	0
DIV vs MIN	1	12:28	2	10	MIN 49	22

Play action crossing routes are an effective way to attack downfield off of play action. Similar to "PA Flood", these plays create a three level stretch and put the hook defenders in a run/pass conflict. This leaves the flat defenders to be stretched vertically.

The play is also a constraint to the naked actions. Paired with the same formations and run fakes, the crossing routes act as a "throwback" off the nakeds. After the play fake, defenders will occasionally turn and run in the opposite direction of the crossing route anticipating the naked concept.

The 49ers got creative with the crossing route coming from the FB/U on the lock-insert block. With lock-insert being one of the 49ers most efficient versions of inside zone, this play action is a great compliment. A good clip of this can be seen in week 16.

This concept is best called vs single high safeties. The defense has a limited ability to get help on the crossing route. Occasionally teams will try to drive the crossing route with the free safety. Week 3 shows a good contrast in clips of how to mitigate this problem. The first quarter clip shows the crossing route coming from an in-line tight end. This takes away the safety's angle at undercutting the crossing route. The 3rd quarter clip shows how the defense can pass these routes off when they come from the outside. The images below show the contrast.

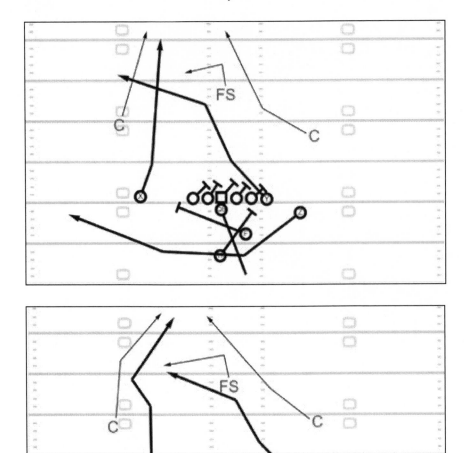

Against two high shells, particularly quarters, the defense has the ability to pass off the deep crossing routes. Against this look, tagging the clear out receiver on a post route (or a "cop" double move) to get over the top of the driving safety can create big plays.

Why it Worked: With the 49ers having great success at running the ball most of the year, they saw a lot of single high coverage on early downs. This leads to big play opportunities for the "PA Cross" concept.

When the defense had a two high safety call on and covered up the deep routes, Garoppolo was able to find his check downs for positive gains in week 6 and week 13.

Why it Didn't Work: The incompletion in week 3 shows how the defense can take away the clear out and deep crossing route out of a single high structure. With larger splits from the receivers, the free safety has the inside track to drive down on the crossing route.

Garoppolo misses an open crossing route in week 17.

In week 15, the Falcons match the routes well from a Tampa 2 coverage.

PA Dagger

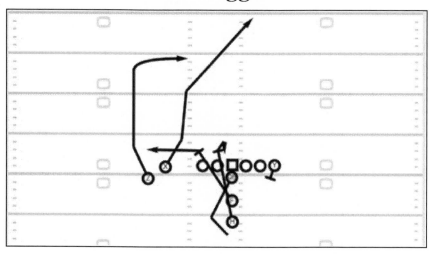

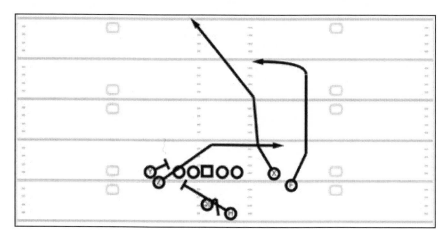

Average Yards per Play	13.3

1st Down		3rd/4th Down (includes RZ)	
Called	Average	Called	Success Rate
3	26.7	0	0%
2nd Down 6-1		**2nd Down 7+**	
Called	Average	Called	Average
1	0.0	2	0.0
Red Zone 10-0		**Red Zone 10-20**	
Called	Touchdown %	Called	Touchdown %
0	0%	0	0%

Cover 1		Cover 2		Cover 0	
Called	Average	Called	Average	Called	Average
3	13.0	0.0	0.0	0.0	0.0
Cover 3		**Cover 4**			
Called	Average	Called	Average		
2	10.0	1	21.0		
Cover 5		**Drop 8**			
Called	Average	Called	Average		
0	0.0	0	0.0		

Week	Quarter	Time	Down	ToGo	Location	Yards
Week 2 vs CIN	3	15:00	1	10	SFO 25	39
Week 3 vs PIT	3	4:33	1	10	SFO 36	20
Week 9 vs ARI	4	4:42	2	11	SFO 25	0
Week 14 vs NO	2	7:29	1	10	SFO 25	21
Week 16 vs LAR	4	12:46	2	7	SFO 21	0
DIV vs MIN	3	14:36	2	5	SFO 42	0

Dagger is another nice way to create a three level vertical stretch off play action. The Dagger concept will create this stretch in the seam, whereas Flood and Cross create the stretch on the sideline.

From the condensed split, the dig route will have inside leverage on the corner. The key from here is the route technique he uses to keep that leverage and create further separation.

Shanahan would typically work the dig route to Deebo Samuel.

Why it Worked: In week 2, Samuel worked the DB's blind spot and gets him turned around. In week 3, Samuel presses the corner's outside hip hard and forces him to turn his hips vertically.

Why it Didn't Work: In week 16, the receiver running the dig route gave up his inside leverage, and had to work hard to gain it back. This gave the DB a chance to play tight coverage and contest the dig throw. In week 16 and the DIV round, the throws to the dig route were slightly behind the receiver as well.

PA Smash / Mesh

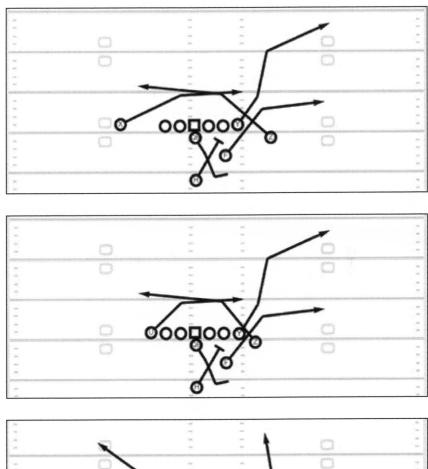

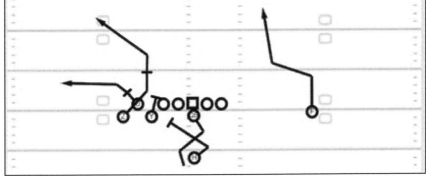

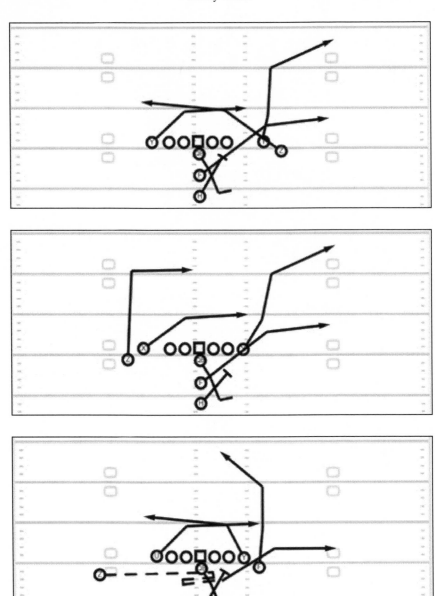

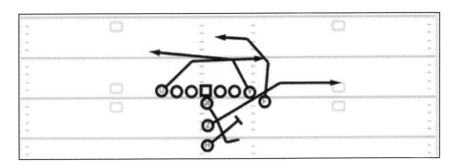

Average Yards per Play	3.7

1st Down		3rd/4th Down (includes RZ)	
Called	Average	Called	Success Rate
1	0.0	5	100%
2nd Down 6-1		2nd Down 7+	
Called	Average	Called	Average
1	2.0	2	5.5
Red Zone 10-0		Red Zone 10-20	
Called	Touchdown %	Called	Touchdown %
4	50%	1	0%

Cover 1		Cover 2		Cover 0	
Called	Average	Called	Average	Called	Average
4	5.0	1.0	5.0	2.0	1.5
Cover 3		Cover 4			
Called	Average	Called	Average		
1	5.0	0	0.0		
Cover 5		Drop 8			
Called	Average	Called	Average		
0	0.0	0	0.0		

Week	Quarter	Time	Down	ToGo	Location	Yards
Week 2 vs CIN	1	11:50	3	2	CIN 43	5
Week 3 vs PIT	2	11:34	1	7	PIT 7	0
Week 7 vs WAS	4	12:27	4	1	WAS 35	2
Week 9 vs ARI	2	2:00	2	7	CRD 11	6
Week 9 vs ARI	3	0:04	4	1	CRD 1	1
Week 11 vs ARI	4	13:03	3	1	CRD 9	7
Week 14 vs NO	4	11:41	2	10	NOR 37	5
Week 15 vs ATL	1	3:06	4	1	ATL 36	5
Week 15 vs ATL	4	10:12	2	2	ATL 2	2

Progression Read:

1. Corner Route
2. Flat Route
3. Drive Route (into QB's vision)

Pairing a high-low smash concept with mesh in short yardage/ red zone is common in most levels of football. This action is the famous "Spider 2 Y Banana" from Gruden's QB camp.

Against man coverage, the natural rubs on the inside make it hard to keep up with the flat route out of the backfield.

A few other low red zone variations were included.

Why it Worked: This action worked very well for the 49ers in 2019. Converting 3rd and 4th downs in critical situations throughout the season. Garoppolo does a nice job of getting the ball out of his hands quickly on these concepts.

Why it Didn't Work: In week 3, the corner does a nice job recovering after the Duo play fake.

Filter Screens

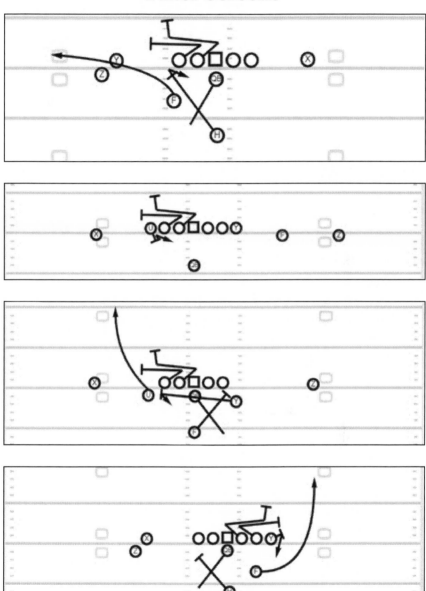

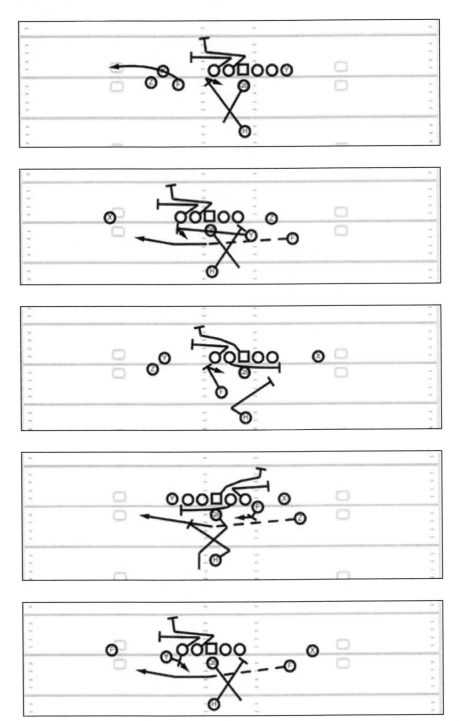

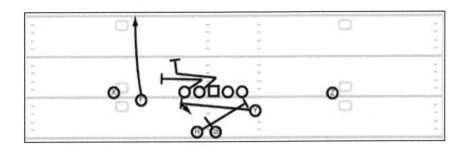

Average Yards per Play	7.1

1st Down		3rd/4th Down (includes RZ)	
Called	Average	Called	Success Rate
7	9.4	0	0%
2nd Down 6-1		**2nd Down 7+**	
Called	Average	Called	Average
0	0.0	7	4.7
Red Zone 10-0		**Red Zone 10-20**	
Called	Touchdown %	Called	Touchdown %
0	0%	3	0%

Bear		Over	
Called	Average	Called	Average
0	0.0	9	8.4
Under		**Mug**	
Called	Average	Called	Average
4	6.5	0	0.0
Wide		**Odd**	
Called	Average	Called	Average
1	-3.0	0	0.0

Week	Quarter	Time	Down	ToGo	Location	Yards
Week 3 vs PIT	2	8:09	1	20	PIT 21	0
Week 5 vs CLE	1	2:33	2	17	CLE 36	-3
Week 6 vs LA	1	14:22	2	9	SFO 18	4
Week 8 vs CAR	1	13:08	1	10	SFO 37	11
Week 8 vs CAR	1	10:33	2	8	CAR 17	15
Week 8 vs CAR	1	3:52	2	11	SFO 24	12
Week 10 vs SEA	3	4:20	1	10	SFO 40	0
Week 11 vs ARI	3	12:30	1	15	CRD 22	19
Week 11 vs ARI	4	13:47	2	10	CRD 18	9
Week 16 vs LAR	2	12:54	1	10	RAM 42	23
Week 16 vs LAR	2	6:47	1	10	SFO 25	13
Week 16 vs LAR	3	15:00	1	10	SFO 25	0
Week 17 vs SEA	2	6:54	2	10	SEA 15	0
Week 17 vs SEA	3	14:22	2	11	SFO 24	-4

The filter screen was a 1st and 10, 2nd and long play call for Shanahan in 2019.

The filter screen seems to be best run to the side of the 2I/1 tech. In this case, the tackle will have an easy time of getting out to kick out the force player, and the center will lead up through for the TE/FB/RB. The diagram below shows the filter screen run to the weak side against an over front.

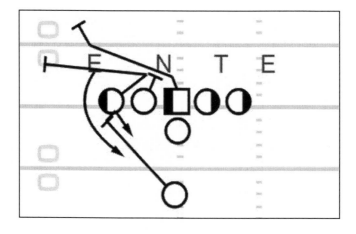

Another great way of running the filter screen is off counter action. The 49ers used this variation a few times with a good amount of success. These variations can be seen in the 7th and 8th diagrams, and are found in both week 11 clips. In both clips, the screen is run to a 3 technique, but the center does a nice job of overtaking him from the tackle. This allows the tackle to still get out for the screen. The counter action also influences the 3 technique to scrape over the top, which makes the centers overtake easier.

The vast majority of filter screens were run against a cover 3 defense.

With all lineman covered vs bear fronts, I would think the 49ers would check out of this call and not have it in the game plan against these looks.

When calling it to the running back from under center, Garoppolo would often use a shovel pass technique and flip the ball.

Why it Worked: Screen production is a trademark of a well schemed and well coached offense. The 49ers used the filter screen well in 2019. Formation and backfield variation prevented defenses from getting a beat on any tendencies.

Why it Didn't Work: Garoppolo couldn't connect with an open running back in week 3 and week 17. The unblocked DE prevented a clean shovel pass. In the other week 17 clip, either the TE gets too wide, or the play side tackle does not get out quick enough.

Slip Screens

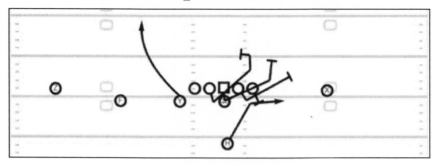

Average Yards per Play	4.3

1st Down		3rd/4th Down (includes RZ)	
Called	Average	Called	Success Rate
10	3.6	5	0%
2nd Down 6-1		**2nd Down 7+**	
Called	Average	Called	Average
2	20.5	8	2.3
Red Zone 10-0		**Red Zone 10-20**	
Called	Touchdown %	Called	Touchdown %
1	100%	1	0%

Bear		Over	
Called	Average	Called	Average
2	5.0	10	5.4
Under		**Mug**	
Called	Average	Called	Average
7	4.6	0	0.0
Wide		**Odd**	
Called	Average	Called	Average
4	1.8	2	0.0

Week	Quarter	Time	Down	ToGo	Location	Yards
Week 1 vs TB	1	6:21	2	3	SFO 28	2
Week 1 vs TB	2	4:28	1	17	TAM 22	0
Week 2 vs CIN	**1**	**2:46**	**2**	**4**	**CIN 39**	**39**
Week 3 vs PIT	1	13:54	1	10	SFO 42	TO
Week 3 vs PIT	1	7:38	3	15	SFO 44	8
Week 5 vs CLE	3	4:31	2	10	SFO 46	12
Week 5 vs CLE	**4**	**13:22**	**3**	**10**	**SFO 22**	**0**
Week 6 vs LA	1	9:17	1	5	SFO 30	4
Week 6 vs LA	2	8:04	2	12	SFO 9	-6
Week 6 vs LA	3	14:51	1	10	RAM 17	14
Week 6 vs LA	4	6:41	3	10	SFO 28	2
Week 7 vs WAS	**2**	**2:31**	**3**	**10**	**SFO 42**	**0**
Week 7 vs WAS	2	1:04	1	10	SFO 45	1
Week 8 vs CAR	2	12:48	2	10	CAR 10	10
Week 9 vs ARI	4	8:39	2	11	SFO 16	0
Week 10 vs SEA	2	15:00	2	10	SFO 26	2
Week 10 vs SEA	4	0:49	1	10	SEA 48	6
Week 11 vs ARI	**3**	**0:26**	**1**	**10**	**CRD 29**	**3**
Week 11 vs ARI	**4**	**15:00**	**2**	**7**	**CRD 26**	**8**
Week 12 vs GB	1	9:26	3	18	GNB 47	2
Week 12 vs GB	1	6:56	1	10	SFO 49	2
Week 12 vs GB	**2**	**10:35**	**1**	**20**	**SFO 18**	**0**
Week 15 vs ATL	1	1:46	2	10	ATL 31	1
Week 17 vs SEA	**1**	**8:37**	**2**	**9**	**SEA 27**	**-9**
SB vs KC	**1**	**9:38**	**1**	**10**	**KAN 25**	**2**

The 49ers will call their running back slip screen out of any formation and personnel grouping. With that being said, only one variation is drawn above.

The front side guard will be the first out on the screen (typically). He will kick out the force player. The center is typically the 2nd guy out, and he will lead up through the alley. The back side guard is typically the "clean up" guy to take any defensive lineman that are trying to chase the play from behind.

The running back is taught to aim for 4 yards outside the tackle.

This screen was used with play action a few times. These plays can be found at week 1 1Q, week 3 1Q 13:54, week 6 2Q 8:04, week 12 1Q 6:56, and week 17 1Q.

Why it Worked: In week 8, the play scores from the 10 yard line. Slip screens can be a good play call in this area of the field. On this particular play, the defensive end goes inside the tackle, and the RB goes outside that block. The guard and center do an awesome job of getting out quickly and staying flat.

In week 2, the 49ers call the screen into the teeth of a nickel blitz. Perfect play call and perfect execution for that specific blitz.

Against 5 man pressures, the play averaged 5.4 yards per attempt. These plays are bolded in the table.

Why it Didn't Work: When slip screens were called on third downs, it was typically long yardage situations with a low conversion probability.

The turnover in week 3 was a result of the running back getting wider than his first blocker. In week 6, the front side guard takes too long getting out.

Throwback Screens

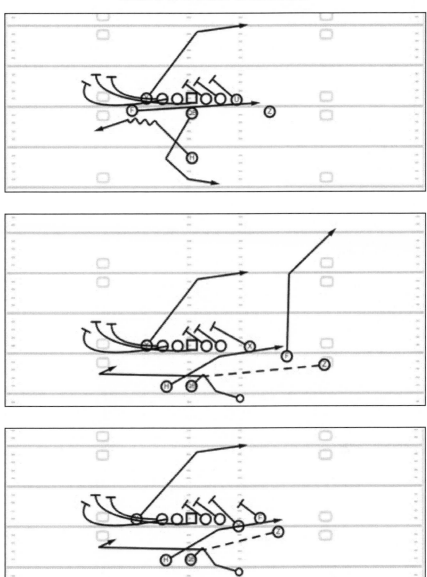

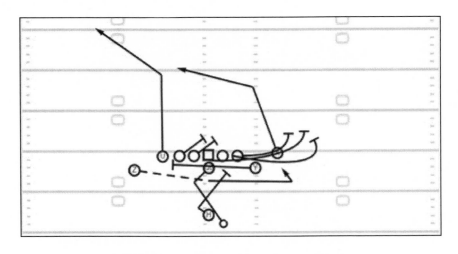

Average Yards per Play	20.4

1st Down		3rd/4th Down (includes RZ)	
Called	Average	Called	Success Rate
3	37.7	0	0%
2nd Down 6-1		2nd Down 7+	
Called	Average	Called	Average
2	-5.5	0	0.0
Red Zone 10-0		Red Zone 10-20	
Called	Touchdown %	Called	Touchdown %
0	0%	0	0%

Bear		Over	
Called	Average	Called	Average
0	0.0	4	21.0
Under		Mug	
Called	Average	Called	Average
1	18.0	0	0.0
Wide		Odd	
Called	Average	Called	Average
0	0.0	0	0.0

Week	Quarter	Time	Down	ToGo	Location	Yards
Week 2 vs CIN	2	6:57	1	10	SFO 25	38
Week 11 vs ARI	2	9:03	1	10	SFO 25	57
Week 14 vs NO	2	3:42	2	3	SFO 27	-7
Week 16 vs LAR	2	13:38	1	10	SFO 40	18
NFCCG vs GB	1	6:48	2	4	GNB 32	-4

Another neat misdirection element to the 49ers offense, these throwback screens are a constraint to their play action nakeds. The offensive line will make the play look like outside zone to the side of the screen.

While only called a few times, they were successful and important part of the offense.

Why it Worked: These screens are a unique way to work the flow back away from the nakeds. In week 2 and week 11, the defense plays man. The offensive line picks up the man defender for the screen and the 49ers pick up big yards.

Why it Didn't Work: In week 14, the defensive end stays home and the left guard has to hold his block for a long time. The play gets blown up.

Tunnel Screens

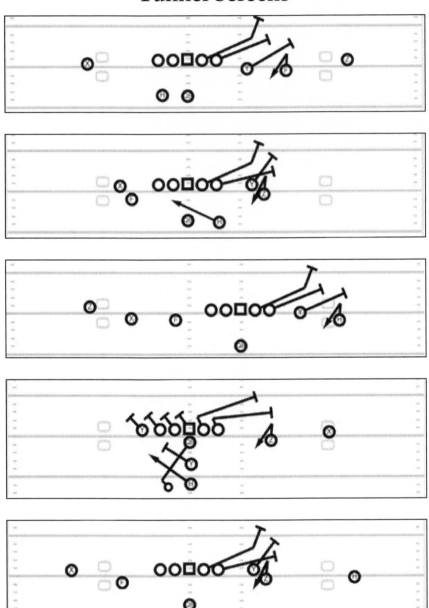

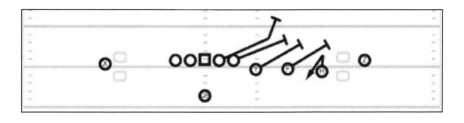

Average Yards per Play	3.6

1st Down		3rd/4th Down (includes RZ)	
Called	Average	Called	Success Rate
7	4.0	6	0%
2nd Down 6-1		**2nd Down 7+**	
Called	Average	Called	Average
1	11.0	5	0.6
Red Zone 10-0		**Red Zone 10-20**	
Called	Touchdown %	Called	Touchdown %
2	0%	2	0%

Bear		Over	
Called	Average	Called	Average
0	0.0	1	-2.0
Under		**Mug**	
Called	Average	Called	Average
2	2.5	2	9.0
Wide		**Odd**	
Called	Average	Called	Average
0	0.0	1	7.0

Week	Quarter	Time	Down	ToGo	Location	Yards
Week 1 vs TB	1	11:50	3	15	TAM 18	7
Week 1 vs TB	2	0:46	2	18	TAM 27	0
Week 1 vs TB	2	0:17	3	18	TAM 27	2
Week 2 vs CIN	2	1:14	1	10	SFO 33	11
Week 3 vs PIT	2	0:50	1	10	SFO 20	-5
Week 6 vs LA	2	2:00	1	10	SFO 16	11
Week 6 vs LA	**2**	**1:25**	**2**	**10**	**SFO 50**	**-2**
Week 7 vs WAS	2	11:39	3	12	WAS 21	0
Week 8 vs CAR	1	2:02	1	10	CAR 18	9
Week 8 vs CAR	2	0:50	1	10	SFO 25	2
Week 9 vs ARI	**3**	**6:37**	**2**	**12**	**CRD 26**	**5**
Week 11 vs ARI	**4**	**2:00**	**2**	**3**	**SFO 42**	**11**
Week 14 vs NO	4	9:10	1	6	NOR 6	0
Week 14 vs NO	**4**	**2:34**	**3**	**16**	**NOR 30**	**7**
Week 15 vs ATL	4	1:59	3	4	ATL 28	3
Week 16 vs LAR	**1**	**8:46**	**2**	**8**	**RAM 8**	**0**
Week 16 vs LAR	4	2:00	2	16	SFO 19	0
Week 17 vs SEA	1	7:51	3	18	SEA 36	7
Week 17 vs SEA	2	0:45	1	10	SFO 31	0

The quick tunnel screen is a nice change of pace play. The offensive line will pass set for two counts, and then look to kick out 2nd level defenders on the side of the screen.

McVay and LaFleur typically reverse the tunnel screen for third and very long situations. Shanahan will use it in that situation as well, but he will mix in it on early downs more.

This screen averaged 4.2 yards per attempt against 5 man and 6 man pressures. These clips are bolded in the table.

Why it Worked: A great block at the point of attack by the closest receiver, as well as a defensive end rushing hard upfield give the offense a chance to pick up good yards.

The big play in week 8 is off of the outside zone play fake shown in the 4th diagram.

Why it Didn't Work: The most critical block is the first block by the closest receiver. The play can typically pick up positive yards if the offense gets movement here. In the cases where the play did not pick up many yards, this block was often the cause.

In week 7, Garoppolo fumbled the snap in the rainy conditions.

In week 15 the man defender triggers hard and tackles Kittle just shy of a first down.

In week 17, the man defender triggered hard on the tunnel action out of quads. Up to this point in the season, the 49ers have only run this play out of quads. This goes back a year years as well. One of the few formation tells in the 49ers offense.

Misc. Play Action / RPO Pop Plays

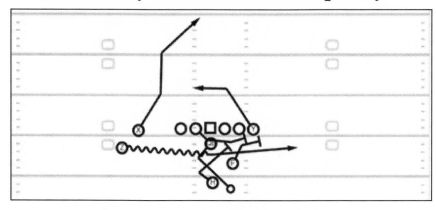

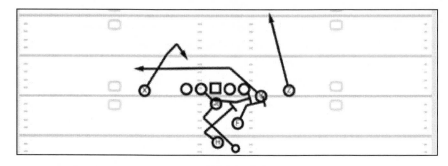

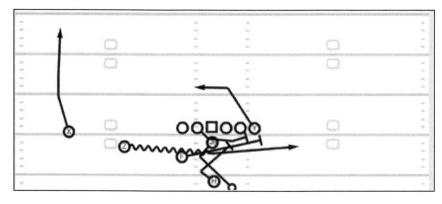

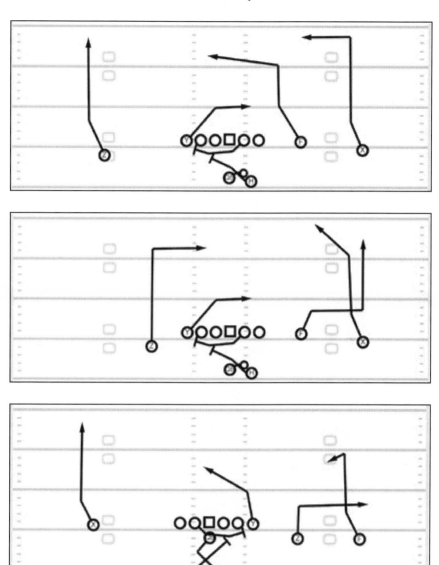

Bobby Peters

ABOUT THE AUTHOR

Bobby currently coaches at York Community High School, in Elmhurst Illinois. You can find more of his work at:

www.theofficialpetersreport.blogspot.com

Email: bpeters1212@gmail.com

Twitter: @b_peters12

Other Books on Amazon

The 2018 Chicago Bears Complete Offensive Manual

The 2018 Los Angeles Chargers Pass Game Index

The 2018 Tennesse Titans Passing Index

The 2017 Los Angeles Rams Third Down Manual

The 2017 Philadelphia Eagles Third Down Manual

The Melting Pot: How to Acclimate Old NFL Concepts into Your High School or College Offense

Quarterback Development: How Four NFL Teams Coached Their Quarterback to Have A Successful 2016 Season

The Complete Third Down Manual: The 2016 New Orleans Saints

Made in the USA
Middletown, DE
04 March 2020